GNARLED LIANAS AND FINE-LEAFED FERNS

ISLETS OF RUSHES IN RIVER SHALLOWS

HERONS PERCHED IN TREES AT NIGHTFALL

TANGLED ROOTS IN A MANGROVE SWAMP

A LONE JACARANDA TREE IN A SEA OF FOREST

ROUGHENED TREE TRUNKS ON A QUIET BACKWATER

THE AMAZON

THE WORLD'S WILD PLACES/TIME-LIFE BOOKS/AMSTERDAM

BY TOM STERLING
AND THE EDITORS OF TIME-LIFE BOOKS

THE WORLD'S WILD PLACES

Editorial Staff for *The Amazon*:
EDITOR: John Man
Deputy Editor: Simon Rigge
Picture Editors:
Jean I. Tennant, Pamela Marke
Design Consultant: Louis Klein
Staff Writers:
Heather Wyatt, Tony Long
Picture Researcher: Kerry Arnold
Art Director: Graham Davis
Design Assistant: Vivienne Field
Editorial Assistant: Vanessa Kramer

Consultants
Zoology: Dr. P. J. K. Burton
Invertebrates: Dr. Michael Tweedie
Botany: Phyllis Edwards
Geology: Dr. Peter Stubbs
Ornithology: I. J. Ferguson-Lees

Published by Time-Life International (Nederland) B.V.
5 Ottho Heldringstraat, Amsterdam 18

Tom Sterling is a writer based in Rome with a special interest in wild life and exploration. He is the author of *Stanley's Way, Exploration of Africa* and *Unity's Children*, the latter about the newly independent states of Africa. He was correspondent in West Africa for numerous English and American publications and has also written scientific works for the Food and Agriculture Organization in Rome. His travels in Africa, Madagascar and the Himalayas have provided the bases for articles and filmscripts. Among his more general writings are two novels, two histories and three thrillers.

Nicholas Guppy, the consultant on this book, studied botany and tropical forestry at Cambridge and Oxford Universities. In the early 1950s, he worked in the forestry department of (then) British Guiana, leading a number of expeditions into the interior on which his book *Wai-Wai*, about the forests north of the Amazon, was based. Since then he has been a lecturer, filmmaker and wild-life consultant. He is the founder of the Primitive Peoples' Fund (now called Survival International).

The Cover: A maze of rivers partitions the tropical forest around the northern headwaters of the Amazon. The subsidiary stream in the foreground has contorted itself into such snake-like loops by never-ceasing erosion and deposition of sand.

Contents

A Wilderness of Forests and Rivers

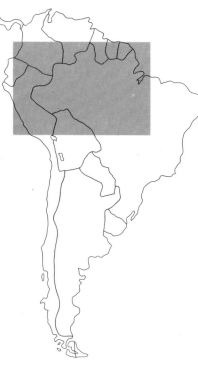

The luxuriant, forest-covered Amazon wilderness (green rectangle above) extends across two-fifths of South America, north and south of the equator. It is bisected by the largest river in the world, the Amazon itself, and networked by no less than 1,100 tributaries. As shown in the detailed relief map (right), most of the region is a flat river basin less than 650 feet above sea level (dark green). This vast area of 2½ million square miles is bounded by the towering Andes in the west (white) and the lower Guyana and Brazilian Shields in the north and south (light green). The boxed area is shown in more detail on page 51. Despite its luxuriant mantle, most of the basin is strangely infertile, and only the four per cent that is regularly flooded (hatched) has rich soils.

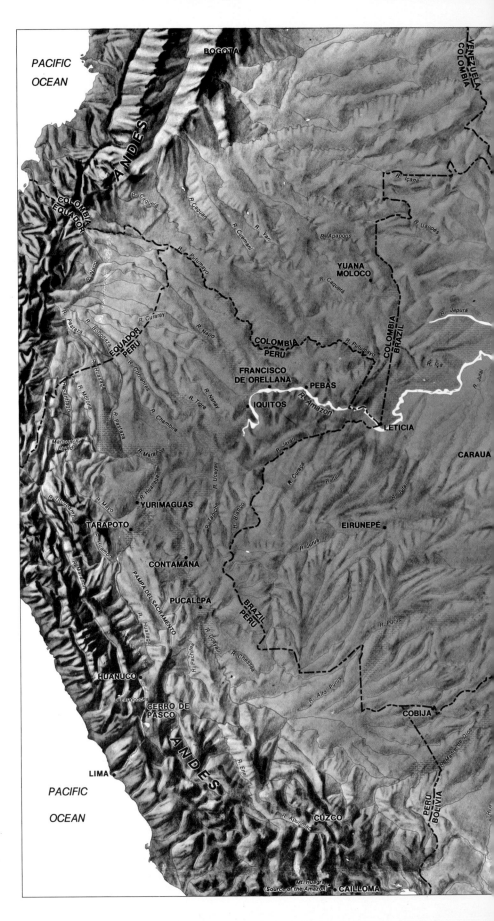

PACIFIC OCEAN

ANDES

COLOMBIA
EQUADOR

BOGOTA

R. Caquetá

R. Caguari

R. Cuenmani

R. Yari

R. Putumayo

R. Napo

R. Apaporis

VENEZUELA
COLOMBIA

R. Içana

R. Uaupés

R. Japurá

YUANA MOLOCO

R. Caquetá

COLOMBIA
PERU

R. Putumayo

COLOMBIA
BRAZIL

R. Iça

R. Jutaí

FRANCISCO DE ORELLANA

PEBAS

R. Curaray

EQUADOR
PERU

R. Napo

R. Nanay

IQUITOS

R. Amazon

LETICIA

CARAUA

R. Pastaza

R. Bobonaza

R. Corrientes

R. Tigra

R. Pastaza

R. Morona

R. Huasaga

R. Chambira

R. Javari

R. Curuca

R. Itui

R. Juruá

R. Santiago

Manseriche Rapids

R. Marañon

R. Huallaga

R. Ucayali

R. Tapiche

R. Branco

EIRUNEPÉ

YURIMAGUAS

R. Mayo

R. Ullucuyacu

TARAPOTO

R. Utcubamba

R. Huallaga

R. Juruá

CONTAMANA

R. Tulumbo

PAMPA DEL SACRAMENTO

PUCALLPA

BRAZIL
PERU

R. Purus

R. Ucayali

R. Pachitea

R. Chesea

HUANUCO

R. Marañon

R. Huallaga

L. Lauricocha

CERRO DE PASCO

R. Alto Purus

COBIJA

ANDES

R. Ene

R. Madre de Dios

LIMA

PACIFIC OCEAN

R. Apurímac

CÚZCO

PERU
BOLIVIA

Mt. Huagra
(Source of the Amazon)

CAILLOMA

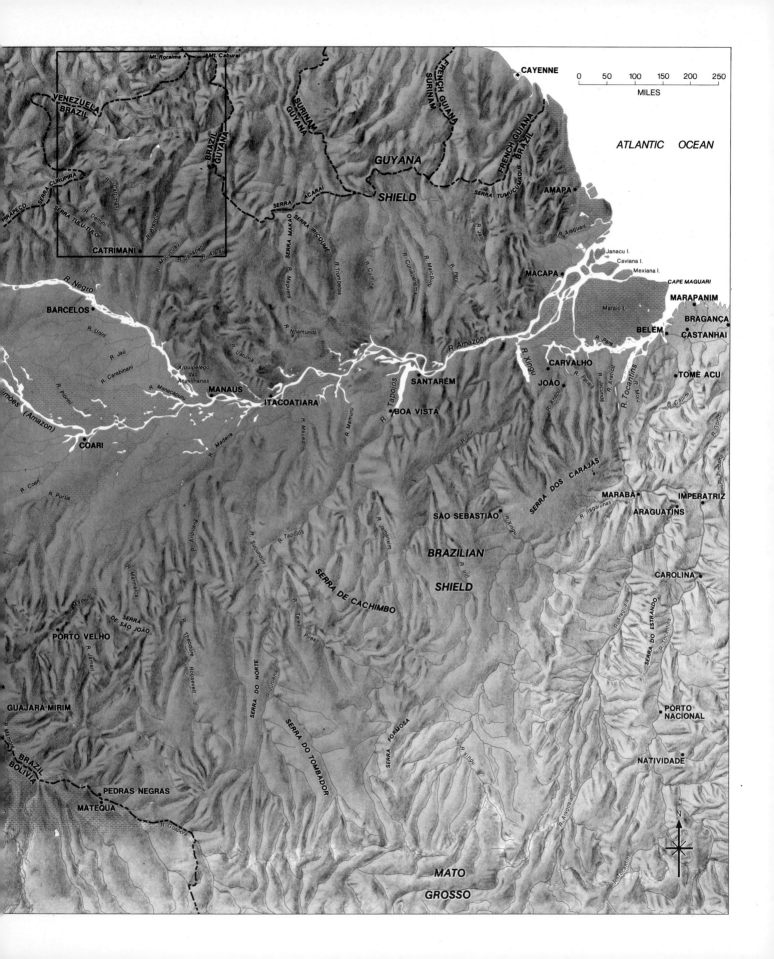

1/ The Many Amazons

Storm clouds began to build up in the pale sky at about half-past three in the afternoon, like blocks of blue-grey ice. On either side of the river, the walls of green vegetation grew sombre and forbidding. There were three of us in a small open boat—myself, a guide and a boy—setting out on a week's exploration into the Amazon region's vast maze of rivers and forests. Hoping to reach the cabin of a solitary rubber collector before the storm broke, the guide made time by taking short cuts. The low jungle banks were flooded to a depth of twelve or fifteen feet, and as long as the light lasted, he explained, we could avoid a number of bends in the river by cutting between the trees. We did this twice, with batteries of thunder shaking the leaves down from the trees all around us, before the lowering sky reduced visibility to ten yards, and we had to return to open water.

The rain seemed seconds away. I was eager for it to come, if only because a storm is that much closer to its finish once it has started. We throttled back to half-speed, feeling our way. The cold slate sky cracked with lightning, the bolts coming straight down on every side without their characteristic jagged shape. As the first few drops scattered around us like huge silver coins, the hut appeared through the gloom. We landed, safely tucked our gear away inside, and stood under the thatch and watched as the storm broke. The sky went purple. The jungle whitened under the lightning, as if lit by the flicker of an ancient arc lamp. With a roar of thunder, the heavens opened and a sheet of water fell between us and the Amazon world. We could barely see in front of us, only hear the savage pounding of the rain and smell the curiously satisfying stench of sodden leaves, logs and earth.

I had seen great storms before, but never one in which so many elements of nature rushed together in a primitive fusion of forces. The sky, the whipping forest, the river became parts of a single, untameable entity. The sight of it brought home the unchallenged supremacy of nature in this forest, and powerfully confirmed the impression I had formed during my first researches: that the Amazon—by which I mean both the river and its forest-covered basin—should be approached with as few preconceptions as another planet.

That much was clear from the raw statistics of the river Amazon itself. It is the greatest river in the world. Rising as a tiny brook 17,000 feet up in the snow-capped Andes of Peru, a mere 120 miles from the Pacific, it plunges down through ravines and gorges and then flows through the vast basin, gathering strength all the time, until finally it floods into the Atlantic, 4,000 miles away to the east on the other side of the continent. It is probably only the second longest river in the world after the Nile (its exact length is still disputed), but by volume—a far more significant measure than length—the Amazon is unrivalled. From its mouth it pours out one-fifth of all the river-water on earth—as much water in one day as the Thames delivers in one year. This torrent drives back the salt water of the Atlantic for over 100 miles. Its mouth is 200 miles wide. Even 1,000 miles upstream, the river is seven miles wide in places and the watercourse is so deep that ocean-going liners can navigate it 2,300 miles inland. The next largest river after the Amazon, measured by volume, is the Congo, yet two of the Amazon's major tributaries, the Negro and the Madeira, each disgorge at their mouths as much water as the Congo.

But the Amazon cannot be understood just as a river. It is a whole wilderness, a great integrated system of rivers and jungles, taking up about half of Brazil and parts of eight other South American countries. Permanently awash with water and sprouting with vegetation, the flat-bottomed basin, rising not more than 650 feet above sea level, covers an area of no less than two and a half million square miles. Viewed from a satellite—for it is impossible to glimpse more than a fraction of the Amazon from an aeroplane—it would appear in the shape of a sauce-boat, with the widest part of the basin, 1,000 miles across, in the west and the narrowest in the east. At the back of the basin stand the Andes, where the sauceboat would have its handle, while the highlands of Guyana bound the north side and the Brazilian highlands the south. These two great rock formations narrow to form a spout leading to the Atlantic, and through this pour the waters of the Amazon.

Glinting through the lush vegetation on the flat floor of the basin are the main river's 1,100 tributaries and smaller streams, branching out and stretching back far into the highlands and mountains. Seventeen major tributaries are over 1,000 miles long—longer than the Rhine, which is one of the greatest rivers in Europe. To the explorer of the Amazon, rivers like the Xingu, the Tapajos, the Madeira, the Trombetas and the Negro are as awe-inspiring as the main river itself. Together they bring down such a vast quantity of water from the snows of the mountains, the springs of the high ground and the heavy rains precipitated by the moist atmosphere above the forest that, according to one calculation, the basin at any one time contains two-thirds of all the river-water in the world. Considering the vast flow of water from the Amazon's mouth, it seems odd at first that so much water should be trapped in the basin. The explanation is simple: the bottom of the basin is almost flat. For 3,000 miles from the base of the Andes to the Atlantic Ocean, the Amazon plain drops a mere quarter of an inch per mile, barely enough to clear a bath. The whole area is almost an inland lake.

So vast and complex is this network of rivers that, ever since Columbus inaugurated the age of discovery in the Americas at the end of the 15th Century, Europeans have found it easier to understand the main trunk as a plural; it still appears on many maps as the "Amazons". Amidst this maze of tributaries, the main river has only recently been traced to its source and the confusion of centuries still leaves its mark. Only the last third of the river is invariably labelled the Amazon. Much of the central section is also known as the Solimoes, and the final section from the western end of the basin up into the Andes has six alternative names.

Dotted through the jungle like tiny islands of civilization are the few towns of the Amazon: Iquitos, Manáus, Obidos, Santarém, Belém. They are all inland ports on the main trunk of the great river and most of them were founded by the Portuguese in the hey-day of their Brazilian Empire early in the 17th Century. Right in the centre of the Amazon, where the river Negro flows into the main river, stands Manáus, as incongruous in the jungle as a block of flats on Venus. It was from there that I set out to discover the surrounding wilderness.

On the day of the great storm, we had pushed our way nearly thirty

A bird-eating spider spreads its seven-inch leg span across the litter of the forest floor. Relying on the wide view from its eight eyes—one of them visible between the front legs—it runs and pounces on its prey rather than catching it in a web in the normal way. Its bite is fatal to small birds and insects.

miles up a tributary of the river Negro, the Cujeiras, north of Manáus. I was introduced almost at once to the Amazon fauna. That evening a giant tarantula entered our thatched cabin, perhaps attracted by the light, or disliking the damp of the drenched forest, or both. Since it was about the size of a soup plate, one of our party moved to kill it. But the man who owned the cabin stopped him. This particular spider was covered with hair, which appeared to be standing straight up, as was my own. These hairs, I learned later, can be dislodged (usually by fear) and can cause great irritation and discomfort to anyone they touch. That might have been one reason why our host did not want the creature killed indoors. There are a number of species of Amazonian tarantulas, but none of them, unless actually poked in the eye, is inclined to bite a human being.

After a leisurely examination of the people in the room—particularly me, as I pushed my rum tea aside—the spider retired. I tied my hammock very high around the cabin poles that night and slept quite unexpectedly well. The next morning the forest was gloriously fresh, with hundreds of subtle shades of green sparkling in the sun.

The incident would hardly be worth noting, except that it revealed a confusion shared by most people, myself included, about the nature of this jungle wilderness. The very word Amazon suggests a Green Hell: forty-foot snakes, piranha fish which will strip the flesh from one's bones, dreadful fevers, ulcerous diseases and centipedes a foot long. Generations of explorers and writers about the Amazon have conjured up this horrific vision but it lacks a strong foundation in fact. Many of the diseases do not belong to the Amazon at all, but have been imported from other continents. And most Amazonian fauna are not very dangerous nor, on land, at all large. I knew all this by the time I arrived in the Amazon, but when I came face to face with the spider, the spectre of the Green Hell had come flooding back. I might have banished my preconceptions intellectually, but clearly I had underestimated my emotional resistance. To make matters worse the spider was nothing in comparison to the sting-ray, the anaconda, the alligator, the piranha and the few other creatures of the Amazon which can be genuinely dangerous. How would I react when faced with one of those? My chance to find out came a few days later.

It was a very hot afternoon. Stopping the boat, the guide suggested we should have a little swim. I asked, as casually as possible, if there were any piranhas in the water. Of course there were, he said, as he ripped off his shirt and trousers and dived in. The other member of our party, the young man, went over the side also. It was a moment of truth. I was left in the position of a new boy at a particularly rugged public school. As in such schools, unspoken scorn soon does its work. I jumped into the river about as eagerly as I would have jumped into the Antarctic waters of the Weddell Sea, and then climbed straight back into the boat. After flopping around noisily for a few minutes, my companions returned and the guide gave me a bare nod of recognition, for which I was pathetically grateful.

Nothing to it, he said, if the river is not actually teeming with piranhas, especially in high water. All one has to do is keep moving—do not float, do not idle. He then told a story of a pilot of a large tourist boat out of Manáus who would take his passengers to a nearby lake to catch a few piranhas (a bird's heart makes a good bait) and would conveniently have engine trouble when they were about to leave. His .accomplice, a strapping cabin boy, would strip to his pants and dive into the water to free the fouled propeller or the blocked water intake. The women tourists sobbed with fear and admiration, while their husbands looked uncomfortable. When the brave lad came back safely, outrageous tips were thrust upon him, which he modestly accepted. The pilot took most of these—but the boy was training to be a pilot himself one day.

It is only fair to add, however, that the circumstances in my case may have been somewhat exceptional, because large populations of this truly dangerous fish were not normally found in this area. I later visited another river where the piranhas were not quite so benign. On one occasion, in a boat, I saw an ugly, black creature about the size of a football bite down on the blade of a hunting knife so hard that its teeth were scattered about like popcorn. But even there, most accidents with piranhas took place in fishing boats—piranhas are good eating—when the fish were hauled in and left to flap around on the bottom. The piranha may then remove a finger or a toe; I saw several nine-toed fishermen. Although the wilder stories of piranhas devouring a beast, or even a man, within a few bloody minutes, are probably exaggerations, it seems wise to treat these fish with great respect.

Still, my quick splash in the river left me feeling that piranhas were not as bad as I had imagined. My confidence increased when the guide told me that caimans—as Amazonian alligators are known—are not usually dangerous either. We saw several on the Cujeiras, in fact, and swam not far from them. They apparently found us unappealing. Even the giant anaconda, the sucuri, which may reach 35 feet in length, is not considered

Sunlight filters into the middle layers of the rain forest, where a hillside breaks up the normally light-proof canopy of the treetops. In the shadows, a silent battle rages as hanging and creeping plants struggle for survival, festooning their fine roots around the limbs of the host trees in a ceaseless search for light, space and moisture.

a great threat to man, although it is fond of embracing alligators.

On later occasions, when I went into the water to cool off (at times this becomes imperative), I only really worried about two creatures, one small and one large. The small one is a tiny fish that can lodge itself in the urethra or the anus, and has barbs so placed that it has to be cut out. The *candiru*, as it is called, actually homes on a stream of urine. The other abiding worry was the giant catfish, which weighs several hundred pounds. This animal, though normally harmless, can grab a foot or half-swallow a man's leg before it realizes its mistake.

Once initial fears and preconceptions about the Amazon are overcome, its reality turns out to be less dramatic than is usually imagined, although infinitely more absorbing. As with any subject, the more one knows, the more one wants to know. But in the Amazon, the process of learning became an adventure in itself. At the end of each day's exploration, as I swung in my hammock with the darkened forest all around me, I found myself being drawn deeper and deeper into the mysteries of this strange wilderness. After the variety of the European world, with its cities and factories, its villages, farms, woods and fields, it was a strange sensation accustoming myself to a land dominated by two features only: water and forest.

The first thing which strikes you is that "land" is not quite a correct description. The floor of the Amazon basin is so saturated with water that many explorers have called it a "river-land". In the Amazon, you do not travel by road but by water. The rivers are the roads of the jungle, 50,000 miles of navigable "trunk rivers" in all, and innumerable secondary streams and creeks. Because the floor of the basin is so flat, large areas of forest are flooded every year or even all year round. Often the river banks are under ten to forty feet of water, and the floods extend for 25 miles or, in exceptional cases, up to 60 miles inland on either side of the river bed. Even when the rivers are not in flood, large expanses of water are left trapped in the undulations of the landscape. These *varzea* lakes, as they are known in Brazil, punctuate the whole of the Amazon basin along the line of the rivers, looking from the air like dark commas in the jungle. In the lower Amazon, from Manáus to the Atlantic, large riverside areas are either very marshy or even flooded all the year round. The land there is so flat that the Atlantic tides flow straight in and out over the marshes without hindrance, as if the spout of the Amazon basin was half submerged in the ocean, and even 500 miles inland the rivers move back and forth in harmony with the ocean.

In this huge river-land it is always raining. The equator passes through the mouth of the river and cuts across the whole region. To the north of it, the height of the rainy season is in June and to the south of it, in December or January. As the rivers rise and subside, first in the north then in the south, the whole Amazon pulsates with water like a giant heart. I saw some of the strange effects of this on the Cujeiras. As we travelled upstream, I was amazed to discover that we were moving *with* the current. The enormous pressure of the river Negro, a few miles below us, was forcing the little Cujeiras to run backwards. The heavy rains to the north had let up only about a month before and the larger northern Amazon tributaries were still shouldering their way past the smaller ones in their rush to the sea. Where the descending waters of the Cujeiras exactly balanced the pressure of the giant river below, we came to an absolutely still part of the river, stagnant as a pond. The water was covered with an inert litter of leaves, blossoms, spiders, twigs, spume and dust. It looked like a marble floor that needed sweeping, faintly reflecting the overhanging forest as highly polished marble might do. As we passed the point of equilibrium, the river at last began to flow weakly downstream, and nature returned to my idea of normal.

But what was "normal" in this extraordinary place? It was really no use constantly trying to impose European norms on the Amazon. Take the forest, for example. It is the largest in the world, and totally un-European in scale, covering an area ten times the size of France. Apart from the delta region, where grazing plains have been cleared, and few dry areas of savannah in the lower Amazon, vegetation cloaks the entire Amazon basin, creeping right up into the foothills of the Andes and overgrowing the sloping sides of the Guyana and Brazilian highlands in north and south. It is densest in the upper Amazon above Manáus. For hundreds upon hundreds of miles, it lines the river banks with a monotonous, sullen greenness, brooding and silent.

It is a world complete in itself, living by its own laws, adapted to conditions which are, if not unique on our planet, at least unique on this scale. To start with, the familiar European landmarks, the seasons, do not exist. There is no summer, autumn, winter or spring, only the wet and dry seasons, which are in any case barely distinguishable in the upper Amazon, and the constant, humid, equatorial heat. At Manáus the temperature averages 81°F, hovering between the 70s and 90s all the year round, year in, year out. Plant and animal life goes on in what to us seems utter confusion. Shedding of leaves, budding and flowering; moulting, pairing and breeding all occur simultaneously. Sometimes after a heavy shower, plants burst into flower as if spring had suddenly arrived. In the middle of the day, the voices of the animals are silenced, leaves droop and petals fall as if autumn had set in. From the almost bitter cold of the forest at night to the freshness of the morning to the languid heat of the afternoon, life seems to pass through a whole year's seasons. And yet, except for a few partly deciduous areas, the forest never turns brown. With all the heat and all the water of the Amazon, vegetation grows and sprouts with constant and extravagant luxuriance, as if protected by a giant greenhouse.

Another strange feature of the Amazon forest is its strange and forbidding darkness. As the millions of trees fight each other for a share of the light, they grow to enormous heights and spread their foliage like a green umbrella at the top, leaving the trunks bare. Only about 10 per cent of sunlight penetrates to the ground and one walks through the forest in a deep gloom with the lofty green vault of foliage far above, as if in a shuttered medieval abbey. In its nether regions, the forest appears to be engaged in a savage but silent civil war. Lianas, tropical climbing plants, wind themselves like boa constrictors round the tree trunks and arch themselves in great loops as they struggle upwards for a glimpse of light. The trees put out roots, which crawl on the ground like serpents, or flank themselves with powerful flying buttresses. Epiphytes, air plants which live off the humid atmosphere or have their own water reservoirs, cluster close to the treetops. It is as if the floor of the forest had been raised on stilts, leaving only the foundations and plumbing to be seen by those wandering below.

This great world of water and forest—unmarked by seasons and only dimly lit—is strange enough. But the picture remains incomplete and still comparatively unremarkable until another dimension is added: time. It is perhaps the Amazon's most extraordinary feature that it has lain relatively unchanged and undisturbed for over 100 million years. To get an idea of what this means, one has to remember that temperate forests, like those in Europe and North America, are a mere 11,000 years old—about one ten-thousandth of the Amazon's age. They grew up after the last ice age, whereas the Amazon was protected by its tropical heat from the grinding embrace of the glaciers. The Amazon is thus one of the last places on earth where one can look deeply into the past— where one can touch a tree and realize that its thin bark, its buttressed roots, its straight, light-seeking trunk are examples of plants still in their primeval state. As I came to know the Amazon, I had the uncanny feeling that I was wandering the earth in prehistoric times, before the emergence of man—or perhaps even exploring another planet.

There are other equatorial forests elsewhere, of course, in Africa and the Far East. But none of them is as big nor as untouched by man as the Amazon. In this vast luxuriant hothouse, the struggle for life among the species has reached a level of extreme complexity. Because the surroundings have been the same for so long, plants and animals have had time to evolve without interruption into innumerable different forms, filling every conceivable niche in the forest's ecology and creating new ones. As a result, the Amazon now encloses a greater variety of highly individualistic species than any other place on earth. Strangely, individual examples of species are very hard to find. They are scattered through the forest in ones and twos, never grouped in stands as in Europe. The pattern is the opposite of what one has come to expect in a temperate climate where single species—the fittest—predominate. In the Amazon, if you see one type of tree in one spot, you must walk miles (if you could) to find another—despite the fact that there are literally millions of those trees in the forest.

What applies to vegetation applies to all other life. Fish, for example, exist in literally uncounted species: piranhas, sharks, sawfish, needle-fish, rays, soles and innumerable others, many of which are sea creatures which have adapted themselves to live inland. Within the Amazon river system there are known to be more than 1,500 different species; by comparison, 500 are found in the Congo and all the rivers of Europe hold barely more than 150. And this disproportion is probably much greater. Recently, an expedition of the British Royal Geographical Society to the Mato Grosso in the southern Amazon region made a collection of fish in local rivers and discovered that about 50 per cent of them were new to science. The people living on the river Amazon usually do not bother to catch the smaller fish, and hardly know what most of them are.

It is easy to see why the first Europeans to visit the Amazon believed that it could support human life almost limitlessly. It seemed a world of inexhaustible natural riches. Early accounts, beginning in the 16th Century, speak of vast herds of sea-cows, or manatees (many weighing well over a ton); shoals of giant turtles boiling in the current; fish which grabbed a line the moment it was lowered over the side, and even jumped into the boat uninvited. No doubt there was some truth in these tales, for even today, after considerable human depredation, fish are extraordinarily abundant, especially during the dry seasons. In the *varzea* lakes along the main river, any amateur can hook a hearty supper within an hour or so. The splendid *pirarucu* grows to several yards, and provides mammoth fillets. The *tucunare* and the *tambaqui* are only about two feet long, but the first tastes absolutely exquisite and the second has a robust flesh rather like sweet pork. The most dangerous of the piranha species—the big black one—is delicious when grilled on an open fire. This probably explains why barefoot, toeless fishermen keep hauling them into boats.

But in a sense one might say that the Amazon betrayed the men who first explored it, for it is far less bountiful than it appears. Although one could gorge oneself on fish in the dry season, there was usually no way to preserve it for the time of scarcity in the wet season except by salting, and salt itself was often difficult to come by. Fruits were occasionally available, but the strange characteristic of the Amazon, that similar trees are often very widely spaced, made them difficult to find. The only staple food aside from salt-*pirarucu*, was *mandioca*, the Portuguese word for cassava, a starch-yielding plant which is native to the Amazon. As the 19th-Century British naturalist, Henry Walter Bates, remarked to a friend, "I have lived on salt fish and mandioca root . . . having mandioca and fish for breakfast, and, to vary the thing, fish and mandioca for dinner." Although there was game in the Amazon, creatures on land tended to be both smaller than those in the water and, as a general rule, less gregarious. They were spread out in the same manner as the vegetation species. Even today the primitive Indians of the Amazon seldom live in groups of more than 60 or 70 individuals, and they roam large areas. They know all about planting and harvesting, and have some ingenious methods of agriculture. But to produce enough food to live on they must wander about their territory like nomads in a desert.

All this should have made the first explorers of the Amazon a bit nervous. From the 18th Century, when the scientists began to arrive, there were increasing doubts about the fertility of the luxuriant Amazon forest. As I continued my exploration of the river Cujeiras, I began to see the reason for their doubts. Only a few families live in the lower reaches, and the upper part of the river is wholly deserted. Most of the people are half-Portuguese and half-Indian—*caboclos*, as they are called in Brazil. They live by gathering forest products and, to a certain extent, by agriculture. But although almost every isolated cabin we passed was flanked by a small cultivated area, I was immed-

These rough-cast pieces of Indian clay pottery, made before Columbus reached South America in 1498, were unearthed by a subsistence farmer near the river Cujeiras and presented as gifts to the author. The casserole lid (top) has an incised pattern still characteristic of Indian pottery today. The head-shaped fragment (above) was probably the handle of another cooking pot.

iately struck by how miserable the plantations were. It would have seemed that in this rich forest, the people could manage something better than scraggly fields of mandioca and a few blowsy palms.

At noon, on the day after the storm, we stopped at one of these cabins to prepare some lunch. Walking up a steep bank of bare earth with a bag of our supplies, I saw a woman coming down to greet us. Several large-eyed children trailed behind her; we never did see a family without a number of children, though there were not many adults—infant mortality is very high.

At first sight, the woman looked quite old. But when I came closer and looked into her eyes, and saw the firm flesh of her arms, I realized she could hardly be more than thirty. She was, I believe, simply tired.

It soon became clear however, that she was by no means a convenient, social-worker's example of a down-trodden peasant woman. One glance from her clear, brown eyes was enough to dispel any patronizing sympathy. She had a commanding presence and could easily have been, in another place, a company executive or a headmistress. Her husband was off in the forest, she said, helping some other men move a valuable log of mahogany down to the river. She offered us coffee, an automatic gesture in Brazil, if there is any in the house at all.

Then she came directly to the point: she asked if we had any medicine for a suppurating sore on one of her children's legs. In fact, I had a small jar of sulfanilamide, which I gave her. As she looked at the jar, I realized that she couldn't read the label, but I told her that it might work, and certainly could do no harm. My Portuguese is quite primitive but, with such a woman, communication is never difficult. She then asked me how much of the powder to use at a time, and whether it could be contaminated by touching it with one's fingers. She did not ask for the instructions to be repeated.

After lunch, I met the woman coming back from the mandioca field near the cabin. Something about the determined set of her shoulders gave her a peculiar grace—a reminder that human beauty need not be unconscious or child-like. She handed me two small bits of pottery—one apparently the incised rim of a cooking vessel, and the other a small head which may have broken from a larger ornament, or handle. Of course, she said, they were useless; but they might interest me.

I doubt if she would have known what "pre-columbian" was—those pieces were almost certainly made before the age of Columbus—but she wasn't very far from knowing, or from seeing, that I would be very interested indeed. She had found the bits of pottery some weeks before, she said, while digging in the mandioca field. From time to time, pieces like this showed up, which almost certainly indicated that there had been an Indian settlement here, long ago, as so much pottery would hardly have been left by one family. In fact, she added, the land just at this bend of the river was not quite as useless as it was almost everywhere else in the area.

I then asked about these miserable plantations. As a general rule, she said, brushing a strand of jet-black hair from her eyes with her wrist, a family could clear a plot and plant crops for two years. Then it was necessary to move on, as the land became exhausted. She leaned down, then, and picked up some of the earth at her feet. As it lay in her hard, fine hand I saw that it was almost pure sand.

This exceptional woman, a person of undoubtedly superior intelligence and resolve, could hardly extract enough from her field—apparently one of the best in the area—to feed her children. Perhaps, therefore, one had to look at these poor plantations not as signs of incompetence, but as proof of man's ingenuity and perseverance. When we left a few minutes later, the woman gave me the two pieces of pottery to take with me. I did not have to tell her that I was extremely pleased to have them. She knew.

Later, in the boat, I spoke to my guide about the apparent difficulty people had with growing food here. He remarked that everyone knew how hard it was to scratch a living from the mighty forest which loomed on each side of us. He did not seem to think that this was a paradox—not any more than it would have been to say that it was extremely unprofitable to grow cabbages in the Sahara.

I was puzzled, to say the least. How could a jungle, especially a particularly lush jungle like the Amazon, so insistently remind one of a desert? As I was mulling over this latest Amazonian mystery, I found myself thinking of Francisco de Orellana, the Spanish explorer who in 1541 became the first European to navigate the Amazon. Reading the journal of the expedition, compiled by Gaspar de Carvajal, a Dominican friar who accompanied Orellana, one can sense a desert-like quality. Carvajal's stories of "royal highways" built of stone, of gleaming white cities, finest porcelain and of "Amazons", fair-skinned women warriors who fought "as ten Indian men", sound almost like mirages. None of these phenomena has been positively confirmed by historians, although evidence of the famous Amazons, who gave the river its name, has been reported by a number of distinguished travellers since and the Indians did have pottery. One can only conclude that Orellana and Carvajal were seeing things, or exaggerating to the point of fantasy. But why? Very possibly their royal highways and gleaming white cities were indeed mirages. On the vast watercourse of the river Amazon, where the banks disappear from sight, islands on the far horizon seem to hover above the surface of the river, and the reflections from the undulating water are known to distort human vision. Recent explorers have reported how a few stucco houses and a church appeared like a city on high red banks, and grazing cows become as large as elephants. Likening the earth's greatest forest to a desert is also not as absurd as it seems, though it took me a great deal more time to understand this.

By now my first, almost unthinking analogy of another planet had become a reality for me. I was really losing my preconceptions and beginning at last to enter the mysteries of the Amazon. Coming back down the Cujeiras one day we stopped at another tiny water-front cabin. This was owned by a family with three children, ranging down from nine to four. The father and the children spoke a bit of Portuguese, though the mother-tongue in the house seemed to be Tupi, one of the 150 Indian languages spoken in the Amazon. The two oldest children (possibly one was a cousin, as they were so nearly the same age) promised to take me for a walk in the forest during the afternoon. They said their names were Samuel and Rachel, though I never knew if this was true or not, because they were both prodigious liars. At the last moment, the four-year-old girl decided to come along too, wearing nothing but a tiny pair of ragged pants and a prominent navel.

Once through a scraggly mandioca plantation behind the cabin, we plunged into the primeval forest. In spite of the fact that it was obviously the children's playground, it was also rather dense jungle, thick with lianas twisted like cables around straight trunks of trees which soared twenty or thirty yards to the green canopy over our heads. There was surprisingly little underbrush, probably because there was such dim light near the ground. The path was obstructed only by giant fallen trees, their buttresses torn up, exposing unexpectedly shallow roots writhing at their bases. Many of the trunks I stepped on were as soft as sponge. And yet most of them clearly hadn't had time to rot; they were riddled by termites. In fact, almost nothing appeared to be rotting; there was no dank or oppressive odour. A *clean* jungle.

The children floated through the forest ahead of me like birds. Even the little one could move much faster than I could. From time to time

Sharp spines bristle in bands from top to bottom of a 60-foot palm trunk. Only the horizontal rings, the scars left by older fronds, are smooth. Palm trees grow sparsely in the deep forest, but are found in large numbers along waterlogged riverbanks.

they stopped so that I could catch up, warning me to be careful of a jaguar behind that tree, a snake hanging from that branch, a spider dangling over my head. As I say, they were terrible liars. But sometimes, just to be confusing, they told the simple truth. "Look!" Samuel said, holding up a leaf which had been cut out like Venetian lace by termites. "Isn't that beautiful!" Not to be upstaged, Rachel said that some yellow mushrooms on a fallen tree-trunk were pretty handsome too. All three of them giggled.

However, there may well have been jaguars somewhere in this jungle. We came on several old traps—really heavy wooden cages which had at one time been equipped with portcullis doors rigged to fall when the cat took the bait inside. They hadn't been used for a number of years and obviously outdated the little cabin on the riverbank. The children liked to play in them, of course, and Samuel growled ferociously from one as I passed.

But after we had been walking for nearly an hour the children evidently grew tired of this game and flitted off to another one. For a while, I could hear their disembodied giggling through the trees; then only their soprano cries, slightly malicious, like 18th Century music. Finally, total silence, except for some birds far above whose chiming voices oddly reminded me of glass shattering on pavement. Not knowing the way on, I decided to go back. But what had seemed a clear path before was now much less so. I must have wandered away from it almost immediately, though I wasn't aware of this for another half-hour or so. By that time, I noticed that my steps were leading downwards, quite steeply. The spongy litter underfoot was also growing damp.

Then I slipped and reached out to balance myself against a tree trunk. Being long-sighted, I didn't notice that the tree—a palm—was covered with thorns. These came off, in rather neat patterns, in my hand. The pain, added to the sudden loneliness of the forest, made the experience suddenly disagreeable.

I continued down, however, and found the expected stream. It was confined to a course only about six feet wide and three deep. To my astonishment, it glowed dark red under patches of sunlight and it was wholly transparent. The bottom was covered with white sand, which acted as a reflector for the sunlight, so revealing the red colour of the water. I did not fully appreciate it at the time, but I had stumbled on a clue to the Amazon's desert nature.

Picking out a few remaining thorns, I knelt down to wash my bloody hand in the cool liquid. There was no noticeable stain in the deep red water. It was as if the landscape itself was bleeding. Furthermore, it was like the blood of a single body, of a creature I had not been able to see up to that moment simply because it was so huge. Suddenly, I was aware that the forest around me was not composed of a number of species gathered together in haphazard fashion. They all fitted together in a strange but somehow quite natural unity.

I stood up and, at that moment, heard a bird high in the green canopy of the forest. Its song began like the crack of a metal whip and ended like a plucked rubber-band. Someone had already told me that this was the *seringueiro* bird, or rubber-hunters' bird. I don't know whether the name came from its song or whether the bird is so called because it is usually found near rubber trees.

I waited, but the bird didn't call again. There was no other sound anywhere except for the rippling of crimson water around a fallen branch. But I now understood—or thought I understood—that the *seringueiro* bird, the jaguars, the buttressed trees, the Venetian lace leaves, the lianas, the snakes and the spiders, and even the giggling children and I, were all part of an overriding pattern. I must make it clear that this was not a mystical, religious feeling. It was simply a discernible fact, no more unusual than the pattern of a fish's scales. What is more, the pattern had been essentially the same for millennia, frozen as if a cinema film had been stopped at a single frame and never restarted. I experienced the curious sensation of living in the present and the past at the same instant. I was at one with the Amazon.

I then took off my clothes, had a wonderful swim, and picked my way back along the path I had come, guided at the last by a setting sun which created a slightly stronger green glow to the west than to the east. I found the children sitting in our boat, trying to sink it by rocking wildly back and forth. They were screaming with laughter and greeted me as though I had been gone for a few minutes and not 100 million years.

34/

A Half-Drowned World

PHOTOGRAPHS BY CLAUDIA ANDUJAR

In 1500, the Spanish sea captain, Vicente Yañez Pinzón, exploring the east coast of the "New Founde World" of South America, found himself in a patch of fresh water some 120 miles out to sea. Puzzled but intrigued, he headed towards land. Picking his way through a maze of islands he entered a continuous stretch of fresh water so vast that he called it simply La Mer D'ulce, or the Freshwater Sea. He could not compute its vast breadth but exploring further inland, he found to his amazement what appeared to be a river 40 miles wide. In fact, he had already come 200 miles upriver from the mouth of the river Amazon, which is so gargantuan that one of the islands enclosed within it is the size of Switzerland. What he now saw was the main trunk of the river.

The full truth is even more staggering. The Amazon, stretching 4,000 miles across almost the whole South American continent, is only one part of a massive system of 1,100 connected rivers which together contain two-thirds of all the freshwater on earth.

In this half-drowned world, water and vegetation are locked in perpetual battle, advancing and retreating with the flood seasons. There is no one flood period. Instead, tributaries swollen by peak rains from March to July in the north and from October to January in the south produce a pulsating rhythm of flooding which, at its most exceptional, may inundate the vegetation downstream for 50 or 60 miles on either side of the river banks. When the silt-bearing flood waters retreat, the vegetation sprouts with renewed luxuriance.

All plant life must adapt to the waterlogged wilderness in order to survive. Along the marshy river banks, trees exist on roots raised like stilts above the surface of the water, with root branches spread wide to give an equilibrium in the unstable ground. Other plants, like the aquatic fern, float on the surface of the water and absorb their nutrients through their leaves. Most flowers have arrived at a different solution: they have abandoned the forest floor and anchored themselves to tree branches where, as epiphytes, they absorb moisture from the humidity in the atmosphere or trap the rainwater they need in their own reservoirs. In such ways plants are well prepared for the next onslaught of the waters.

Islands of luxuriant vegetation lie like jagged ribbons across the vast river Tapajos, silk-like at dawn. In February, when this photograph was taken, violent rains put an abrupt end to six months of the dry season along the Tapajos, which flows north from Central Brazil to join the Lower Amazon at Santarém. As the water rises, the banks of grasslands are partly submerged and water-loving tropical vegetation sprouts everywhere.

A maze of islands (above), on which trees are seasonally submerged up to their crowns, obstructs the river Negro at its confluence with the Amazon near Manáus. The islands are formed over long periods from sand deposited by the Negro as it is slowed by the greater mass of the Amazon.

Rapids (right) agitate the water of the river Negro near the edge of the ancient, granitic Guyana Shield, which forms the northern boundary of the Amazon basin. Up to this point, 450 miles from the Negro's confluence with the Amazon, the river is fully navigable despite its sand bank obstructions.

44

On the river Solimoes, ghost-like trees, temporarily asphyxiated by a lack of oxygen at their roots, rise above still-thriving vegetation. From November to June, the Solimoes, the name given to the Amazon above Manáus, is subjected to deep flooding from tributaries swollen by rains in the highlands of Ecuador and Peru. Their waters annually raise the Solimoes by some 55 feet, creating a maze of inundated forest on either side. Only as the waters recede down-river does the drowned vegetation begin to burst back into life. The first sign of the rebirth of the trees is the sprouting of the pink buds (right).

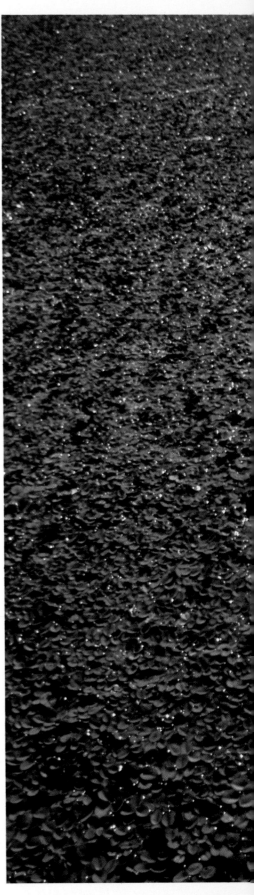

Impelled less by the imperceptible incline of the river basin than by the massive waters that feed it, the Amazon (above) flows towards the Atlantic. At its maximum upstream width of seven miles, when its further bank is lost from view, it looks like a gigantic inland sea.

Thousands of Salvinia (right), a species of aquatic fern, form a leafy carpet over an igapo, where the Amazon has permanently overspilled its banks. The fern, which has dispensed with roots and absorbs nutrients through a specially adapted leaf, grows in profusion on the still waters of the igapos.

2/ The Luxuriant Desert

The waters are as the lands they flow through.

GALEN/2ND CENTURY A.D.

I did not realize it at the time, but when I discovered the dark red waters of the forest stream during my lonely forest walk near the river Cujeiras, I had stumbled on a clue to the Amazon's desert nature. One of the most startling features of Amazon rivers is that they have different colours. For centuries, explorers have returned from the wilderness speaking of white rivers and black rivers, and I had been impatient to see them for myself. In fact, while one can call a river white or black, this is to oversimplify. Once in the Amazon, I quickly found out that white rivers are usually dirty yellow, rather like thin pea soup. And what are called black rivers have water that I saw as red. Although in any considerable quantity they do indeed look black as pitch, they have a red base and when seen in the bed of a shallow stream or held up in a glass, they look like strong tea or even Coca-Cola. Moreover, they are surprisingly transparent, for in the Amazon black is by no means synonymous with dirty, just as white does not signify clean. On the return journey from the Cujeiras to Manáus, I had a swim in the river Negro—the archetypal black Amazon river and the only one actually named after its colour—and I could see my legs kicking below, down to the knee. When I dived beneath the surface with my eyes open, I seemed to be looking through a cut ruby, and shafts of sunlight struck down with gem-like precision all around. As I stared down into the depths, the red turned to deep brown and then, further down, to black. After a few moments, though, the water began to sting my eyes, indicating that it is strongly acid.

In addition to the yellowish-white rivers and the red-black rivers, there are still others that are blue-green in colour, and even clearer than the black rivers. This colour coding reveals a simple geographical pattern that leads to an understanding of Amazon geology.

All the major white rivers (with the exception of the Branco) are found in the western bulge of the Amazon basin and can be traced back into the Andes; the white Ucayali leads back to the official source of the main river itself, which is also white. The black rivers are the river Negro and some of its tributaries, and also some minor tributaries of other rivers rising south of the river Amazon. Most of them drain the highlands of north-west Brazil and Venezuela and flow down southwards into the main river. The meeting of the Negro and the river Amazon is an extraordinary sight. As the white water coming down the Upper Amazon meets the black water of the Negro, the two flow side by side with a clearly visible boundary between them. Only after about 50 miles does the greater volume of the white waters triumph over the black.

The blue-green rivers, such as the Tapajós and the Xingu, drain the Brazilian highlands in the south and flow northwards into the river Amazon. Both the black and blue-green rivers have clear water and come from the ancient rock formations that enclose the Amazon basin to north and south. The reason for their clarity is an almost complete lack of material in suspension. They are among the purest waters in the world, and one can lean over the side of a boat and drink as confidently as one would from a tap. The same applies to rivers flowing south from the Guyana highlands which are generally more turbid, often a muddy green colour; chemically, they have more in common with the blue-green and the black rivers than with the white ones. All of the rivers coming from the north and the south are uncommonly poor in minerals necessary for life. This can only mean one thing. The Guyana and Brazilian rock formations on either side of the Amazon basin are so ancient and tough that the rivers and streams flowing over them grind them down very slowly. Or one could put this another way: whatever was to be ground out of them easily has already disappeared.

The reason for the rather unappetizing pea-soup appearance of the white rivers, on the other hand, is that they are heavily laden with silt and soluble soil nutrients. They contain so much that, according to Frederick Katzer, a German hydrologist working on the Amazon at the turn of the century, a thousand million tons of material in suspension pass into the Atlantic from the mouth of the Amazon every year. With

Below their meeting at Manáus, the silt-laden waters of the Amazon in the upper half of the picture (left) flow side by side with the black, cloud dappled waters of the river Negro. The dividing line between the two rivers, clearly visible in the close-up above, is noticeable for some 50 miles downstream. The Negro carries virtually no silt, because the soils of the ancient Guyana Shield in which it rises have been so leached by millennia of rain that virtually nothing remains to wash into the river except the humus that causes its black colour.

commendable teutonic thoroughness, Katzer then sat down and calculated that this was equivalent to what could be carried by 9,000 trains a day, each with 30 ten-ton trucks.

All this betrays a great deal about the Andes. Since the white rivers flow down from those mountains, the silt must be coming from there. This can only mean that Andean rocks are much softer and therefore younger than either of the rock formations to the north or south. They are, in fact, at least 1,000 million years younger.

To understand this juxtaposition of old and new, it is essential to know the geological history of the Amazon. It is a fascinating story: it also holds the key to the mystery of the Amazon's implacable nature.

The astonishing fact that first has to be grasped is that the Amazon once formed part of another continent much larger than today's South America. Hundreds of millions of years ago, the Amazon rock formations and mountain chains linked up with those of the great primordial super-continent of Gondwanaland in the southern hemisphere. With Antarctica as its heartland, Gondwanaland embraced South America, Africa, India and Australia. The convex east coast of South America then nestled in the concave west coast of Africa, and what is now the mouth of the Amazon was an inland area adjoining the Ivory Coast. There was an Amazon river even then, but it flowed westwards as the shape of the present Amazon basin clearly suggests. The basin is narrow in the east, where the upper reaches of the river would have been, and widens for a long way westwards, as rivers do toward their mouths.

This primordial Amazon geography was disrupted about 140 million years ago when Gondwanaland was gradually torn apart by powerful forces deep down below the earth's crust, and the pieces drifted away to become the present continents. According to the current geological theory, the earth's crust consists basically of two rock layers. The bottom layer is basalt and girdles the entire globe, forming the ocean floors and providing the foundation on which the continents rest. The continents, consisting of lighter granitic rock, are the upper layer and they ride upon the basalt substratum rather like rafts floating on the surface of water. They could quite accurately be described as the scum of the primitive earth.

Over tens of millions of years, powerful currents in the earth's molten centre welled upwards, cracking both the basalt layer beneath Gondwanaland and the covering granite layer of the primordial continent itself. As the subterranean currents forced upwards, they created a ridge in the basalt substratum, forcing those parts of it on either side to move outwards. Since South America was riding on top of the western part, it slowly sailed away westward as an island continent, leaving behind it a gigantic, widening crack that became the South Atlantic Ocean. However, as it moved, it came into conflict with the Pacific Ocean floor which was spreading towards it under the influence of similar forces thrusting up from beneath. When the two met, aeons later, something had to give, and the result of this collision between shifting segments was the present landscape of the Amazon.

Two kinds of rock were involved in this great geological transformation. Like all continents, South America consisted of the ancient rock core of granite and other crystalline materials, toughened by compression and intense heating within the earth's crust, and areas of younger rocks, laid down by sedimentation or volcanic activity. It was this latter sort of younger rocks, at the mouth of the ancient, westward flowing Amazon river, that took the brunt of the collision with the Pacific Ocean floor. As the continent rode over the ocean floor, the younger rocks crumpled in a series of giant folds and contortions, so creating the Andes Mountains. These new, high mountains blocked the mouth of the old Amazon river, and a vast fresh-water lake formed in the west.

Just when all of this happened is in some dispute. Probably the process of folding began as early as 100 million years ago. But the Andes almost certainly took a long time to grow to their present height, and some scientists suggest that they are still growing. One is accustomed to think of scientists as precise servants of the Truth. No doubt they intend to be, but for a number of years staid scientific journals have been publishing rather short-tempered articles about the age of the Andes. One school holds that the mountains rose in comparatively recent times, and another that their genesis took place much earlier. Part of this argument centres around the existence (or non-existence) of a sea-horse in Lake Titicaca, high in the mountains. The sea-horse comes from the Pacific and its presence in the lake would indicate a recent upfolding. One scientist has even spoken rather sharply of a "hearsay seahorse".

Whatever the exact date, it is clear that the basin of the primordial westward-flowing river was made into a lake. For as long as this basin of old sedimentary rock was filled with water, new sediment was being carried into it by the multitude of Amazon tributaries, trapped and accumulated to a depth of several hundred feet. Some time in the last 50 million years, the Amazon fresh-water lake was drained and the sediment at the bottom became the flat floor of the present Upper Amazon basin. The draining was caused by another continental movement. Like rafts rising on the crest of a wave or dipping into the trough, continents can ride higher or lower on the earth's substratum, and tilt in the process. This is what happened to South America. The entire continent tilted towards the east and the waters found an exit into the Atlantic through the narrow gap between the Guyana and Brazilian shields, so emptying the fresh-water lake and forming the Amazon basin of today. Even now at flood seasons much of the Amazon basin is so logged with water that it is not difficult to imagine it as a lake.

Those geological changes that were still to come occurred quite recently. The first happened a mere three million years ago—the day before yesterday, geologically speaking. Ever since South America broke off from Gondwanaland, it had been an island continent, completely separated from North America, which had drifted away from Europe some 60 million years earlier. Then, what had been a string of volcanic islands between the two continents was transformed into a continuous causeway, the Isthmus of Panama. For the first time in perhaps 60 million years, a land bridge was provided across which plant and animal species could migrate to and from North America. The fact that this land bridge was established such a relatively short time ago means that during the preceding tens of millions of years the South American forests and their inhabitants were evolving practically without outside interference, much as another piece of ancient Gondwanaland—Australia—had done.

The latest geological event of any note came during the ice age a million or so years ago. The Amazon basin itself escaped glaciation, but tremendous quantities of precipitation were impounded as ice in the polar regions instead of returning to the sea; as a result the level of the South Atlantic was lowered by at least 300 feet, and the greater drop at river mouths speeded up the Amazon rivers so that they gouged deep channels in the soft sediments filling the basin. When the ice melted, the sea rose again, flooding the river mouths and the huge delta of the river Amazon to such an extent that many of the deeply excavated river beds in the Lower Amazon are now below sea level (though of course most of the water is above). It also turned the mouths of many of the Amazon's major tributaries, such as the Tapajos and the Negro, into great lakes, some so wide it is almost impossible to see across them. The rivers themselves slowed down, and began filling with silt again.

When I went to the Amazon I particularly wanted to explore the oldest parts of the region, the ancient rock shields north and south of the river basin—to walk through parts of Gondwanaland, as it were. Like the basin, great parts of these old shield areas are covered with the richest and most extensive forest on earth. But, unlike the basin, they are frequently cut off from commercial river traffic by falls and rapids. In fact, some areas, especially to the north, are almost completely isolated from European civilization. They much more closely resemble the Amazon as it was before the first Europeans came than do those parts of the basin that are reasonably accessible to boat traffic. Unfortunately (for my purposes) the shield areas contain rich and as yet untapped mineral deposits. And anyone who wants to see land that is both uninhabited and potentially a source of great wealth must expect his motives to be misunderstood. I suppose a person who wanted to investigate Saxon ruins in the vaults of the Bank of England would run into a few problems too.

I had to get permission for my journey from the FUNAI, the Fundação Nacional do Indio (National Indian Foundation). This organization controls all the areas where Indians are living, including those with mineral deposits. It is headed and, in many branches, staffed by commissioned or retired army men. While such regulation seems a reasonable precaution, both to protect the Indians from European frontiersmen and the Europeans from warlike Indians, the officers of the FUNAI are not concerned solely with Indian problems.

At the FUNAI regional office that I visited, I met a general who felt especially protective towards the aborigines for metallic reasons. He was most forthright about it. He leaned across his well-polished desk and asked me, with the slyness of a barrage of field artillery, if I was interested in geology. I replied that I was, though I was not a specialist: the subject interested me largely to the extent that it had helped shape the Amazon environment. But this admission had an electrical effect on the general. I felt like a student whose headmaster has just found a book under plain cover in his satchel.

The general came around his desk and flooded me with a sea of invective. I gathered that he was unmasking me as a mineralogical spy. The interview lasted quite a while and, during it, I had time—a good deal of time—to reflect that if I really had been a spy of this sort, the general's stabbing gestures towards his wall map were giving me a very good idea of some interesting places to visit.

By the end of the interview, I had been discouraged from visiting some regions I had planned to see, though later communications I had with the government about this intention were entirely cordial. Unlike my general, most Brazilian functionaries are very competent indeed, especially when they are being discouraging. But I was at last given permission to visit the upper part of the river Catrimani, a tributary of the river Branco, which in turn flows into the river Negro. As it turned out, the location was ideal: it was well up into the northern shield area and very effectively isolated by rapids; its vegetation and its animal life were almost completely undisturbed by the outside world; and the few Indians living there were among the most interesting to be found in Brazil. The place I had chosen to visit largely for geological reasons turned out to be equally fascinating for botanical, zoological and anthropological reasons. This was not really a coincidence: the Gondwana shield rocks had effectively guaranteed it. To every subsequent question I had about the Amazon, I found at least some of my answers here.

The only way to reach this wild area by land is to run the obstacle course of the river Catrimani, which has no less than 20 rapids, several of them impassable at certain times of the year. Luckily, I managed to get a lift in one of several Indian canoes which were taking supplies from the junction with the river Branco to an isolated missionary far upstream. There were four men in my boat, two pure Indian and the other two of mixed race. They had already navigated these occasionally dangerous waters and knew them quite well. I was most grateful for this, since an inexperienced traveller here can find himself in great difficulty. Every time we came to a long stretch of rapids, the supplies and the boats had to be manhandled round through the forest. At the shorter rapids, however, we paddled on regardless. It was not a relaxing experience, at first. To me, the rocks in the swirling water looked like hungry black teeth. It was not pleasant to remember, either, that with a crushed boat we might as well have been stranded on another planet. The jungle on each side of the river was almost wholly impenetrable, at least for a European. I began to think I should have taken these stories of a Green Hell more seriously.

As we came to an especially ugly section of the river, the Indian sitting in front of me raked his vermilion-tipped arrows backwards in the boat and just missed skewering my thigh as he began to paddle furiously (I wondered if these arrows were also tipped with curare). As I watched the rippling muscles in the boatman's shoulders, I felt the forward pressure he transmitted to our craft. We climbed, inch by inch, through the hissing waters between two vicious stones. At one

The wild forests on the northern edge of the Amazon basin near Brazil's border with Venezuela (green area on inset map) are almost completely cut off from the outside world. Here, the flat floor of the basin (dark green) gives way to the higher terrain of the Guyana Shield (light green) and the broad, navigable rivers narrow into streams barred by dangerous rapids.

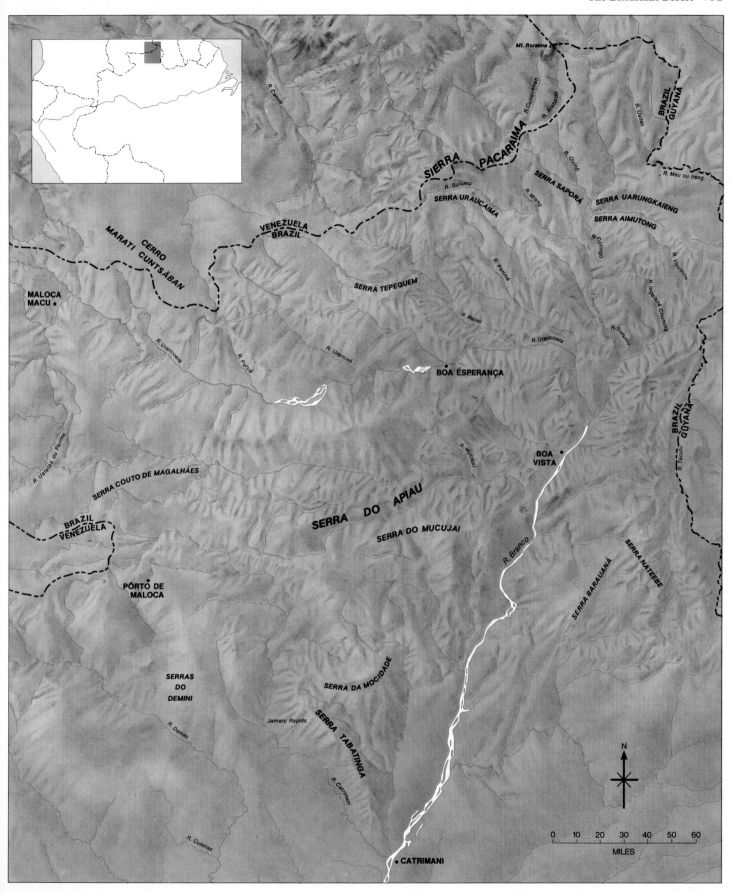

MALOCA
MACU •

CERRO
MARATI CUNTSÁBAN

R. Caroni

R. Uraricoera

R. Puriús

R. Uraricaá

VENEZUELA
BRAZIL

SIERRA   PACARAIMA

Mt. Roraima

R. Cunguenan

R. Arabopó

BRAZIL
GUYANA

R. Uailan

R. Quinó

R. Mau ou Ireng

SERRA SAPORA

R. Surumu

SERRA URAUCAIMA

R. Miang

SERRA UARUNGKAIENG

SERRA AIMUTONG

R. Cotingo

R. Virequim

SERRA TEPEQUEM

R. Parimé

R. Ingalasè Churima

R. Majari

R. Uraricoera

R. Surumu

BOA ÉSPERANÇA

BRAZIL
GUYANA

R. Mucajai

BOA
VISTA

R. Taciutú

R. Uailas ou Parima

SERRA COUTO DE MAGALHÁES

BRAZIL
VENEZUELA

SERRA   DO   APIAU

SERRA DO MUCUJAI

R. Branco

SERRA BARAUANÁ

SERRA NATEEBE

PÔRTO DE
MALOCA

SERRAS
DO
DEMINI

R. Demini

SERRA DA MOCIDADE

Jamaru Rapids

SERRA TABATINGA

R. Catrimani

R. Cuieiras

N

0 10 20 30 40 50 60
MILES

• CATRIMANI

point we seemed to be balanced on a giant, rotating bubble. Then, with a final thrust, we were across into calm water. There had been no paddle for me to use, and my hands were clenched white on my knee.

To my surprise, none of the other men in the boat seemed to consider the experience all that adventurous, or to feel that we had been staring into the Jaws of Death. They did not even seem winded, and in a moment had resumed their previous desultory conversation, sometimes calling across the water to the two other boats that had also made the passage. We might have been paddling through a pleasant, unspoiled park. Raucous macaws, aerodynamically designed like supersonic jets, flew overhead. A black bird about the size of a pheasant rose from a green-bearded rock at the centre of the channel and disappeared into the dark forest. Behind us, the rapids sounded like steam being released from a giant turbine; the noise merely accentuated the green silence of the world we were passing through.

It occurred to me, then, that if the men with me in the boat had been locked into cars and sent hurtling down the British M1 or a West German autobahn, they would have turned to whey with fear. Nor would their reaction have been mistaken. Up to a point, danger is a relative matter. Past that point . . . well, we all know what happens past that point; and my friends were sufficiently experienced to know that we were still safely short of it on the river. Nevertheless, the point exists—on the Catrimani or on the autobahn.

As we continued upstream, we did not see animals gazing from the river banks with the unwary innocence that might be expected in an untouched wilderness. They are not that innocent, and probably never were. Despite the sparseness of wildlife, however, there were enough game-birds on the Catrimani to feed us. A party of 20 to 30 people with a few guns would have little difficulty finding food here. On the other hand, if they stayed for very long, all the game would retreat. No doubt it was partly for this reason that our party shot only a few birds and took a modest number of fish. No one shot at game that would be lost, or could not be used immediately. Shells for the guns were just too expensive, which was obviously another reason for economy. The Indians with us did not risk their arrows on anything but a sure shot either—in fact, they did not risk their arrows at all as long as anyone was willing to risk a shell. They tend to be very cagey about such things. They pointed out the game (they always saw it first) and then waited. Afterwards, they did not mind at all helping to eat it. With bananas and a store of mandioca flour to go with it, we were adequately fed. But we were not overfed, nor ever would be. The jungle had taught the Indians, and was also teaching us, to be as economical as French housewives proverbially are.

I finally asked the man ahead of me in the boat if his arrows were tipped with curare. He had a red feather thrust through the lobe of his left ear, and parts of his body were painted with red juice pressed from seeds of the *urucu* plant. We spoke largely with sign-language, not only because he had no Portuguese but because he held a great, drooling plug of tobacco under his lower lip. I pointed to the leg he had almost spitted and then to the red-tipped arrows, almost as long as spears. He quickly understood what I was saying and rolled back on the gunwales, apparently helpless with laughter. Looking nervously at the plug of tobacco, which somehow stayed in, I laughed back.

I gathered the man was saying that if the arrows had been tipped with curare, it would have been a good joke on me. On dry land, I'm sure he would have given me a tooth-loosening slap on the back. In fact, the Indians here have a rather crude sense of humour. But they laugh at their own misfortunes as much as those of other people. It is the kind of laughter that just brushes another feeling. This is a very rough country, and provides a rough life—and they know it.

We came at last to a smaller base camp, where supplies had to be unloaded from the boats in order to carry them through the forest the following day, past one difficult set of rapids. The boats would be hauled up empty. There were a few Indian women here; they had already lit fires by their hammocks against the approaching chill of the evening. The men proceeded to string up their hammocks also, and I followed their example. After dinner, we all retired. Because the day, here near the Equator, is almost exactly equal to the night, everyone goes to bed at about 7 p.m. and gets up at 5.30 a.m.

Not that people sleep all that time. The Indians spent several hours talking and laughing (relating the day's disasters, perhaps) across their fires. It soon became clear, also, why each one had built his own. It grows quite cold in the forest at night, or the damp makes the chill very penetrating. Even wearing my extra shirt and a light raincoat. I was shivering.

And there were noises. A bird that sounded like someone swinging on a rusty old spring; a whistle, which finally broke into a sparkling waterfall of sound; frogs (they grow as large as boxer puppies) croaking in regular time, like the pulse of the river; the hissing rapids.

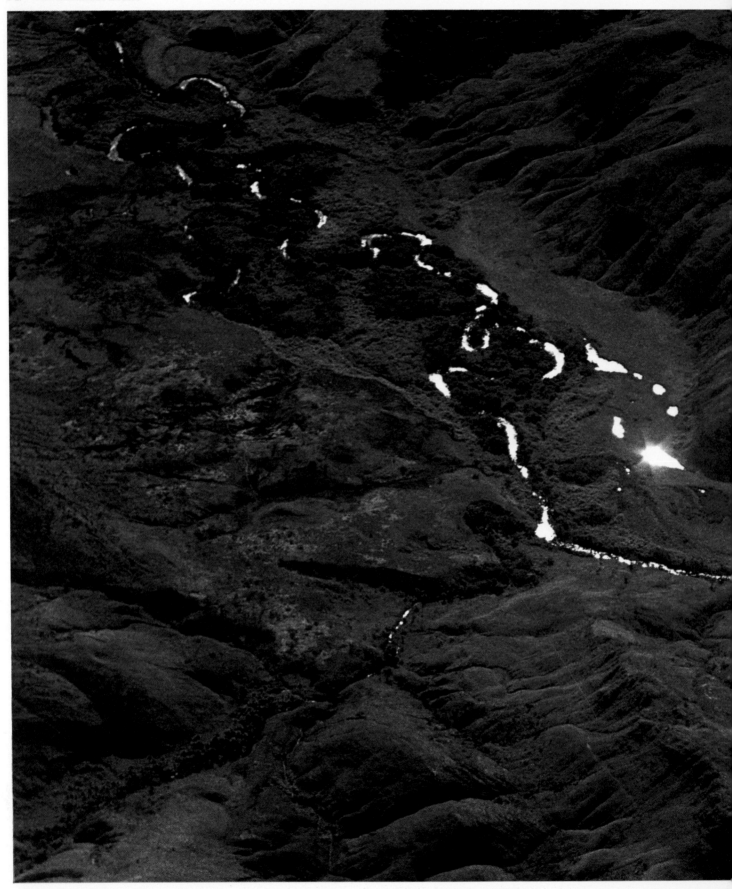

An early morning sun glints on a black-water river rising amid the weathered contours of the Guyana Shield near Mt. Roraima.

Occasionally, a deeper sound from the depths of the forest, perhaps an animal, not at all menacing. And, most disturbing of all, an enormous, outer bell of silence, which all the other sounds only magnified. Drifting off to sleep, I imagined that this muffling silence was time itself, stretching all the way back to a period when nothing even remotely like a human being existed.

There was something uncanny about this feeling, because it was so precisely in keeping with the landscape in which I found myself. These ancient rocks, now lying beneath the forest, had been continuously weathered for scores of millions of years before the emergence of man. Examining the top soil the next morning, I was not altogether surprised by its appearance. It was like bleached sand, and it looked as if it had been washed over and over again. In fact this is very close to what had happened. In the very wet conditions of the tropical climate of the Amazon, persistent intense rainfall dissolves everything soluble in the soil and carries it downwards. This process has gone on so long that the soil is leached of the minerals that are essential to fertility, and only some less soluble, less useful material is left behind.

Up in this ancient rock shield, and especially around the headwaters of the river Negro not far west of here, this leaching has carried to lower parts of the soil even the remains of the less soluble material, creating a bottom layer of mixed humus and metals, mostly iron. It is nearly black. Where a stream cuts through to this "podsol", it picks up these useless minerals, and according to Dr. Harald Sioli of the Max Planck Institut in West Germany, it is this process that is responsible for colouring the black rivers of the Amazon. I had now followed the clue of the black waters to the end. Their colour is a signal given by nature that the soil is exhausted and that few of the fertilizing nutrients essential to life can be found here, either in the water itself, along the river banks washed by the water or in the lands from which the water comes.

It is not surprising that the ancient soil crumbled from granitic rocks should have been leached of nutrients: it has been weathered over many millennia. However, one would expect the debris of more recent rocks to be richer. In the Upper Amazon, the sedimentary bottom of the old fresh-water lake—the so-called *terra firme* area—is only about 30 million years old, while the narrow valley of the Lower Amazon is a mere one and a half million years old, the age of most soils in Europe. And yet none of the comparatively young sedimentary lands are rich at all. They, too, have been leached so long and so thoroughly by the heavy tropical rainfall that they contain few nutrients.

In areas where the sedimentary floor of the Amazon basin is exposed, the combination of heavy rainfall and persistently high temperatures produces an even more refractory type of leached soil called laterite. In this case, the upper surface soil left behind after leaching is quickly washed away, leaving nothing but thick, reddish brown sheets of tough clay. The name laterite, derived from *later*, Latin for brick, comes from the practice in tropical climates of slicing this clay into blocks that harden under the sun into building bricks. The name is extraordinarily apt. Even with a pickaxe it is impossible to break through the pavement-like surface of laterites in the Amazon.

There are, of course, some fertile lands in the Amazon. But apart from some strips of marine sediments, deposited millions of years ago into the sea round the old island continent and now found at the margins of the lower valley, the only genuinely fertile regions are the regularly flooded plains, or *várzeas* (a Portuguese term meaning flat or cultivated). They flank the white-water rivers for between six and 60 miles on either side, and regularly receive the Andean silt that gives these rivers their colour. This sediment is rich in minerals, because it has only recently been detached from its parent rocks, but the fertility of the *varzea* depends to some extent on the way the river flows through. When flowing water is not imprisoned between steep valley sides—and in the flat bottom of the Amazon basin it is not—it tends to meander. The river swings from side to side, undulating like a snake, and in doing so its currents slow down and drop their loads of silts. The effect of this meandering is both to widen the flood plain and constantly to spread nourishing silts. Since the silt is constantly being replenished by the river currents, rainfall and river water cannot leach away all the nutrients. These areas, potentially very fertile, are a very small part of the Amazon basin. They probably cover from 60,000 to 100,000 square miles, less than four per cent of the total area of the basin. In the midst of the greatest forest on earth, men have to huddle around the flood plains because they, laden with rich white silt, furnish the only land that is consistently fertile.

NATURE WALK/ **The Guardian Rocks**

PHOTOGRAPHS BY CLAUDIA ANDUJAR

The San Antonio falls on the river Jari are just one of hundreds of falls and rapids that stand as sentinels on the Amazon's tributaries between the sedimentary basin and the rocks to the north and south of it. I had already travelled up beyond these sentinels in my attempts to understand the Amazon complex of rivers and forests and I wanted to take a look at the guardian rocks themselves.

First in a power boat and then in a canoe, my photographer, Claudia Andujar, and I spent several days travelling up the river Jari and in exploring these falls. The Jari is comparatively small as Amazon rivers go, a bit less than half the length and possibly half the volume of the Rhine—a mere trickle in the mighty flood that rushes to the Atlantic. The falls at San Antonio, which stretch several miles across the river valley in many separate cascades, are not far from the tributary's meeting with the Lower Amazon, because the sedimentary basin narrows to a neck here at the eastern side of the continent and the rock shields approach the central stem of the river.

The trip upriver was oppressively monotonous, almost like moving through a huge tunnel. There was simply nothing to be seen on either side but endless walls of trees, silent and sullen. From a distance, their varying shades of green gave almost the impression of marble, veined here and there by the dark trunks of lianas.

Journey into Time and Space

When we arrived at the falls after a day's travel it became clear that this had been a journey into time as well as space. Waters have been roaring over this black rock (or rock like it, for the falls have obviously retreated as the rock lip crumbled) into clouds of their own mist since the era of the great reptiles. The silent forests were here then also, not too different from their present form, eternally regenerating. Except for the existence of a near-by settlement of brazil-nut collectors, this scene of falls churning over the rock and down through the jungle could have been viewed by the first human beings ever to live in the Amazon.

The rock itself is igneous, that is, once molten rock that was forced into the overlying layers, solidified and has since become worn away. It is almost jet black—"hell black" as a brazil-nut collector put it—

PODOSTEMEAE ON MAIN FALLS

hard, with a high proportion of iron and magnesium. It is this quality that has allowed it to survive for such aeons.

On first impressions, however, one forgets those vast reaches of time. The first morning after we reached the falls opened virginally, as fresh as an uncurling leaf. The delicate rock plants of the podostemeae family bowed submissively as the water pounded around them. There is, of course, no real submission: these plants have been bowing in just this fashion for tens of millions of years. Indeed, they have proved to be a good deal tougher than the rock. They have even eaten holes into it to get a firmer grip. As long as the water and sunlight endure they will continue in endlessly reflected biological images of themselves.

The photographer stood in the bow of the boat, threatening to capsize us all; the steersman was in the stern; I dabbled in the water, caressing the slimy fronds of the podostemeae.

A Traveller on the River

It had been quite chilly when we started out, but as the sun rose the water began to reflect its heat. A traveller on the river is exposed to a much greater variation of temperature than one in the forest. This is no doubt the reason why one never finds these rare podostemeae, which are highly sensitive to changes of temperature, except at falls and rapids, where they are constantly bathed in the river's mist. They are among the most specialized plants in the world. In human terms one might say that they are like men who can survive only on certain streets, in certain cities, on rainy days in August. And yet so unchanging has their habitat been that they have stubbornly held their own where hardier species have perished.

It was now comparatively low water on the Jari and the podostemeae flowers could bloom. In high water the plants are often completely submerged. The flowers therefore follow the dry and wet seasons; bearing seeds when the river is low, which fall on to the hot rock and germinate when the river rises again.

The podostemeae are probably

LIANA SEEKING SUNLIGHT

related to the epiphytes of the Amazon forest. Normally, of course, epiphytes grow on other plants, but I saw several that have adapted to survive on rock. Many of them have developed foliage resembling that of seaweeds or lichens. One sort looks like a cabbage leaf, leathery green on top, leather red and fitted with clinging legs on the bottom. Without flying spray or foaming rapids, however, the intense, reflected heat of the river will kill them (as it would the podostemeae). I cut samples of a number of different epiphyte species and laid them out to dry in the direct sun. Within an hour they had shrivelled to husks. In fact, they are almost entirely made of water, and plants several feet long will reduce to a few fibres barely sufficient to fill a cigarette.

CLINGING WATER DROPLETS

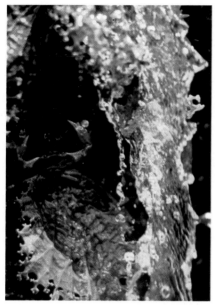

FRESH-WATER CRAB

cies apparently had. Possibly it lived on the larvae of insects, which are also specialized for just this environment and are thus plentiful in the river near the rocks.

The most troublesome insects, as far as I was concerned, were the pium flies, members of the Simulidae family, which thrive near turbulent water. They are almost invisible to the eye, but they leave drops of clotted blood on the exposed skin, which then begins to itch violently.

It was now approaching noon around the main San Antonio falls, and was growing quite hot as one might expect. Clouds were constantly passing overhead, and the mood of the scene changed restlessly. Be-

cause of the dramatically changing light the colours of the river and its vegetation were drab at one moment and brilliant the next. This is particularly true near the falls: when the sky darkens, the spray draws colour from forest and river, and refracts the light into rainbows. One can come within picking distance of flowers without seeing them, until a theatrical ray of light strikes their delicate white and lilac blossoms.

The subsidiary falls of the Jari stretch across the entire valley from east to west. Falls have a natural tendency to spread out, of course, because the rocks that form them tend to dam the water. To a certain

The more robust vegetation of the forest intrudes here also. Lianas invade from the margins of the river, not because they are thirsty for water but because they are searching for sunlight. Almost all Amazon vegetation has this in common: water and light are its first requirements; it can do without soil if it has to. As a result, there is an invasion of life on the river which at times can nearly obliterate the water, especially when plants have rocks to crawl across. It makes for an irresistible blending of forms.

Tiny Crustacea

And, of course, animals follow vegetable life. Tiny crustacea live among the water plants. I saw a member of one of the many species of fresh-water crabs in the Amazon. These are not normally adapted to fast flowing streams, but this spe-

SHALLOW-WATER FLOWERS

RIVERINE UNDERGROWTH

extent, the encroaching vegetation also forces the falls to spread, augmenting the pressure of the rocks. Thus, both plants and rocks tend to push water aside and form land. To get from one falls to another, one must take the boat around islands of tangled jungle.

The vegetation on the banks of the Jari and on the islands between the various falls has more varied shades of green than I have seen on any other Amazon river. This may be due to the fact that the soil beneath the forest is unusually varied also. From a point a few miles downstream, one passes from the sediments of the old Amazon fresh-water lake, to much older marine deposits and, at last, to

LEGUMINOSAE

the crystalline rock. Possibly the chemical changes of the soil have some effect on the colour of the foliage, and partly account for the fact that one finds a slightly greater variation of plant forms here. In any case, riverine vegetation is always richer than that of the monotonous deep forest because it has greater access to light.

Giant House-Plants

In an odd way, learning to see a heterogeneous tropical forest, composed of hundreds and even thousands of different species, tending to look alike, is like learning one's way around a big city. In big cities individuals are also highly specialized in their work; and there, too, a stranger can hardly tell one from another. For the newcomer to the forest, the most immediately recognizable type of growth is the liana. Climbers can reach any size between that of a ship's hawser and that of a common house-plant gone mad. In fact, some, like the convolvulus and the philodendron *are* giant versions of house-plants: they are probably the original forms of our climbing plants. Although lianas compete with the trees, most of them do little harm. They may even be useful in holding large trees up, and it is possible that they encourage the scattering of species which, among other things, may prevent the spread of plant diseases.

Afternoon is the best time to be on the river. Shortly after three o'clock, the sun's rays begin to slant and it becomes fairly cool, especially near the spray of the falls.

We had cut into a narrow, walled channel of the river where the water churned so swiftly it was difficult to keep the boat from spinning around. When one looks at the forbidding rocks here it would seem that the river had chosen to run over the toughest rocks possible. (Of course, water always finds the easiest way down, and beneath the dense forest cover on either side of us were far harder rocks.)

The river rocks, which create not only the San Antonio falls but also a formidable series of rapids beyond, make this area practically impassable. A party of government geologists had just arrived, heading up over the falls. They had several tons of equipment and they intended to be gone for months, travelling at most a few hundred miles

DESCENDING LIANA   *AROID LIANA*

VOLCANIC FALLS

constantly loading and unloading their equipment as they crossed the rapids above the falls.

Above San Antonio, there are the few shacks of brazil-nut hunters; after that, there are no men at all. If there were ever any Indians here they have all been driven out. This whole region was once the fief of a rubber baron who held the few inhabitants along the river's banks in virtual slavery. He was killed in the first decades of this century when the workers rebelled. Since the rubber boom the region north of the falls has remained almost deserted simply because it is so impractical to harvest anything beyond these rocks, and bring the produce to market, paying wages that any free man will accept. Only slave labour, or something very close to that, is profitable.

VERTICAL SHRINKAGE PATTERNS ON IGNEOUS ROCK

The igneous rock at this point has obviously been breaking off from the wall of the falls for ages, leaving debris at the sides of the channels, which the jungle is in the process of reclaiming. From here, I crawled on to what appeared to be a high island in the middle of the river, but which was really nothing more than a great pile of rock, filled in with loose, sandy soil. It was thick with vegetation, including several striking trees with slender red and russet leaves, resembling poinsettia, looking quite out of place among their dark green neighbours. The island was undoubtedly flooded during high water, and seeds washed down by

IGNEOUS DEBRIS

the river had invaded it. In this way, the huge Amazon forest is fused by its water, regardless of the soil beneath it.

Milky-Green Water

Surrounded by milky-green water, ageless black rock, podostemeae and other strange vegetation changing colour under the shifting afternoon light, I might properly claim this as one of the loveliest afternoons I have ever spent. In a way, it surely was. But to be quite truthful I must say that there was an undertone, here, of something unpleasant. It is a feeling one often encounters in the Amazon and it is very difficult to set down in words.

I believe it comes from a visceral awareness that man is simply not welcome here. When surrounded by the comforts of civilization, we think that these sparkling waters,

SILVER-LIT PODOSTEMEAE

BURST OF SUNLIGHT

these primal rocks, these green mansions of the limitless forest will accept us. But once there, there comes a moment in really wild country when one loses one's assurance. That black column of rock wreathed in thundering mist could as easily fit into a nightmare as an idyll. The soaring birds could peck out one's eyes, the fish could eat the flesh from one's bones—indeed, the hordes of insects are already doing so.

A Release of Spirit

This is not to say that one does not encounter great beauty and release of spirit in places not made for man; on the contrary. But with the world's forest areas shrinking to ill-kept parks we tend to idealize nature. An absolute wilderness must be something unpleasant as well as pleasant—and it can never be what we expected it to be because it is the very antithesis of our civilized world.

Evening was now coming on and it was growing chilly. As the light grew dimmer the photographer pushed closer to the crashing waters. Only the thought of ruining her camera (it is well known that when photographers drown the last thing that goes under is the camera) kept her from shoving us right under the torrent. Approaching the falls closely, I noticed that a wind had sprung up, though the entire day had been windless. Then I realized that the volume of water crashing down from the rock ledges overhead was creating the draught, much as a quickly running bath

It was also a disturbing day: I realized that there was practically no way that man could naturally insert himself into this hellish paradise. It gave no quarter. It would not play our game. The rocks forbade any but the most primitive passage farther up, and the peculiarly spread-out nature of the forest made it impossible to gather its fruits in any rational way.

Suppose, for instance, one cut a valuable log of mahogany: it would certainly do the forest no harm, since another would take its place. But how could one get it downriver? And, with each tree so widely separated from one like it, how could one find enough trees to make cutting them down a profitable operation for outside investors?

JAGGED RAPIDS

shower will suck in the curtain around it. And, as we seemed on the point of being sucked in also, I suggested—or rather shouted—that we turn back. But at this point the afternoon light began to play tricks. The sky would grow nearly dark at one moment and then the water would be lit by a burst of dying sunlight. That sort of thing inflames the most sensible photographer, and this one was blazing with enthusiasm. For all the effect my warnings had on her, I might as well have dived over the side of the boat and swum back to shore, and probably would have done so if I had dared. Altogether, the display was magnificent: a crashing, theatrical finish to one of the most beautiful days I have spent.

CRASHING WATERS

HILLSIDE RAIN FOREST ABOVE FALLS

And yet, inevitably, man would continue to search for other ways to exploit the land. The government geologists, who had arrived for several months' exploration of an area only a few hundred miles square, were already doing so. Parts of the rock shield are known to be rich in manganese and iron, among other metals. The rocks which for so long have protected the forests and the wildlife in them may, ironically, become the reason for the forest's eventual destruction.

Later, before dark, we walked along the sides of the falls. Water sometimes rilled from the tumbled rocks, and vegetation made them slippery. But I was glad to be out of the boat and to stretch my aching legs.

Early Indian Carvings

I thought of the botanist, Richard Spruce, who had spent 15 years in and out of such boats on the Amazon rivers. On rocks somewhat like these he had found some early Indian carvings, possibly centuries old. One would have thought that the Indians would have wanted to record their impressions of the great waters and the forests they lived in. Instead, painstakingly and with the most primitive tools, they had incised pictures of their kitchen implements in the rock, showing how they made their bread. They knew—and know—as much about the Amazon as anyone ever will; yet they ignored the threats posed by animals, insects, climate and disease and left behind a clue to its greatest danger for man: hunger.

MAIN FALLS IN FADING LIGHT

3/ Nature's Hothouse

Everything is embroiled in one immense fertilization, one immense digestion, in one immense excretion.

CLAUDIO VILAS BOAS IN LUCIEN BODARD/*MASSACRE ON THE AMAZON*

The Amazon jungle is not everyone's idea of a jungle, with a tangled undergrowth that turned 19th-Century explorers into popular archetypes armed with machetes. In fact, most of it is not tangled at all. Under the high canopy of the treetops, it almost resembles a covered park, with ample spaces and well weeded paths. It is not difficult to imagine that it has been put out on contract to an army of domestic cleaners, all of whom follow the inhabitants around constantly clearing up after them. It is an extremely well regimented forest.

Since in most people's mind a luxuriant forest is virtually synonymous with dense undergrowth, there would seem to be a contradiction here. Nevertheless, paradoxical though it may seem, the Amazon is both neat and luxuriant, as I was soon to discover. When I set out to explore during my canoe journey up the river Catrimani, I hoped to find the explanation. And I was also looking for the answer to another question. How, if the Amazon soils are bleached to the point of exhaustion, does a luxuriant forest thrive on them? In the event, I did discover the answers and once again concluded that although the Amazon is often less dramatic than expected, it turns out to be more absorbing—and demanding—too.

When morning came to our base camp on the Catrimani, my Indian friend shook my hammock not very gently and implied laughingly that it was time to rise and shine. He had got a new plug of tobacco tucked under his lip, and he was as completely dressed as he ever would be. Everyone else was up and moving about. I crawled out of my cocoon and began stamping some circulation into my legs. As anyone who has tried it knows, sleeping in a hammock is not as easy as it appears to be, and I only really got the hang of it towards my last weeks in the Amazon after a great deal of practice.

The men of the camp had scattered through the forest to strip bark from a particular kind of slim, straight tree. The freshly peeled bark they gathered gave off a strong citrus odour, and it seemed to have nearly the tensile strength of steel. The strips were to be used in headslings to carry the party's packing cases through the forest while the boats were hauled up along the bank past the rapids. While this was going on, I intended to slip away into the forest with my still unanswered questions.

After a quick breakfast I accompanied several men who went ahead to decide a route to a calm beach above the rapids. As we moved away from the river I quickly became aware of the lack of underbrush. There was no accumulation of rotting vegetation, and there were none of the miasmal, fetid odours that one might expect in deep jungle. The layer of leaves underfoot was not very thick, hardly more than an inch or so. The leaves were brown but they did not appear to have been there very long. It was impossible to know how long the trunks of fallen trees had been lying there, but almost none of them had been dissolved by rot, as they often are in European forests. Instead, they were shot through with holes, and many of them contained nests of termites. Often they crumbled to dust practically at the touch: most of their bulk had already been digested.

By fortunate accident I came on still more evidence of good house-keeping in the forest. Not far from the camp a sort of informal toilet had been established. The Indians never used it—they wandered off by themselves in the jungle—but the half-Europeans did, and I did too. Behind one particular log, which I remembered, there had been some faeces the evening before. In wandering beyond the camp I mistakenly stepped over this log at the very instant that I recognized it. The mistake should have been disagreeable, but the faeces had almost entirely disappeared. Several times later—on this trip and on others—I noticed that matter of this sort seldom remained much more than 24 hours. It simply vanished. So did other organic refuse. The result was about the cleanest camp I have ever seen.

What is more, I never saw a dead animal in the forest, or any trace of one, except for the empty shell of a turtle on one occasion, and the bare skeleton of a rather large snake on another. I learned that the Indians here customarily tie the dead in the trees. Within about two weeks there is nothing left but the polished bones. They even tie on the jaw with a special bark fibre, more resistant than flesh, to keep it from falling off when the gristle disappears.

Although there was comparatively little underbrush, a good many branches had to be cut away so that the Indians could get through with the packing cases. Some fallen trunks across the path had to be chopped away also; a loaded porter just could not step over them. When the trail was cut, some of the men went back to take the boats round the rapids. A few of the remaining men, together with the Indian women, prepared to carry the supplies overland, so I helped them load the cases in slings. The only other place I had seen headslings used was in the Nepalese highlands. Loading up in mountainous country is fairly easy, because the porter can place the burden on a rock and get his back under it, which is the tricky part of the operation. Here, with no elevated places, the porter sat down, while I lifted from behind. Then the head-slings were attached so as to steady the load. The women, who were mostly just young girls and no higher than my chest, stood while I placed bundles and packing cases on their heads. Some of the larger cases must have weighed over 150 pounds, but the girls waddled away with a graceful yet awkward gait, as if wading through deep water.

After a while, it dawned on me that I was the only loader in the group. Although it would have been quicker for the Indians to help one another with the loading, the job had been given wholly to me. The Indians seemed to think it more fitting that I should do it. They stood around laughing—rather pointedly, I thought.

I really wanted to go off and explore the forest, but I remained a little longer to help two Indians carry a pair of heavy poles. These would be used as a sort of bridge to load the boats again. Half-way along the route I notice the poles were growing extremely heavy. I soon saw the reason. My companions had crouched and dipped their shoulders leaving me to carry the whole burden. Angered, I dropped the poles, which just missed crushing the foot of one of the men. Surprisingly, my anger was not returned; instead the men just leaned against the trees, laughing nearly to the point of tears.

At last I got the message. I was not needed or expected to work. Probably I should have guessed this from the beginning; I just was not sensitive enough. The people did not dislike me—at least they had chosen an amusing and harmless, if spirited, way to get their message across—but obviously, I was expected to keep my place. I was not one of them and never would be. I saw that to them I could have been a member of another species, not a relation of the selfsame one. So I quit (much to the Indians' evident relief) and escaped to the forest surrounds. As I moved away from the river, I noticed that it became even easier to move. There were now relatively few obstructions that I could not quite easily walk around. Many European forests are harder to penetrate. The reason is that there is so little light on the forest floor that scrub growth is unusual. This is true of primary forest—forest in its original state—and it was this sort in which I now found myself. Only when the forest is cut, and the mantle of tall trees removed, does a tangle of undergrowth and small trees—secondary forest—appear.

As I walked through the gloom, I saw that the uniformity that is so obvious from the air—the forest looks like a monotonous green ocean— was no mere surface impression. All the trees, of whatever species, looked alike. It was like visiting London on an improbable day when everyone, no matter what his work or position, had chosen to wear a bowler hat and carry a tightly rolled umbrella. The leaves of the trees, for instance, though of various types, were almost all the same; dark green, large and almost without indentation. They looked much like European laurel leaves. Some that were ready to fall were brown; some new leaves had a reddish colour; but these were exceptions.

My concern for the problems of the forest as a whole was suddenly interrupted by a minor, though intriguing, feature of rain-forest trees. I was so busy looking upwards that I tripped over a huge buttress, a thin, triangular plate of wood in the angle between a tree trunk and its root. These buttresses—there might be three to ten of them radiating out from a tree trunk—are a feature of many rain-forest species. I struck my obstruction impatiently with my stick; it rang with a sound like the bass strings of a piano.

As I walked on, I pondered the reason for buttresses. What was their function in the rain forests of the world? Those I had encountered were not very large—up to one yard in height and several yards long horizontally. But I knew there were areas where the trees had buttresses up to 12 or 15 feet in height—a marvellous game of hide and seek could be had round just one tree. They are sometimes also used by travellers as walls for shelters. The obvious thought is that they support tall trees, much as architectural buttresses support buildings, taking the tree's weight in the shallow soil. Not so: trees with buttresses are blown down just as easily as unbuttressed trees. The trees are more securely supported by the vegetation that dangles between them, and even that is not much of a support: I came to a buttressed tree that had fallen and had pulled a whole collection of vines and lianas with it. The tree had very few roots; all were shallow—less than a yard deep—and there was no tap root. The exact use of these spectacular growths is not known, but they probably fulfil some function of nutrition and moisture gathering.

The tree trunks were, like the leaves, nearly identical, though they varied a good deal in size. The bark was so thin that I could easily cut through it with my small pocket knife. It was usually a greenish white, somewhat mottled. Practically without exception, each tree that had attained a diameter any larger than my forearm soared high into the air, without a branch until the very top. Those with very thick trunks—greater than my thigh—reached much higher with crowns hidden from view. Each trunk was so straight that it might have been turned on a lathe. Bowlers and umbrellas would not have looked more strange.

The trees are not, in fact, all of closely related species. There are differences, but it takes a keen eye to notice them. A brief glance shows colour and texture to be the same; a closer study shows subtle but significant variations; if you smell or actually taste the wood, you realize that there are literally hundreds of kinds of trees in any one part of the rain forest, with the individuals of any one species widely separated from each other.

This uniformity between species is understandable enough. It is a response to the wider uniformity of temperature and rainfall. The air is always warm in a tropical rain forest, though, as I had discovered at Manáus, the thermometer rarely climbs above blood heat.

The second vital factor in the rain forest is, of course, rain. The sky is seldom clear and the rain falls frequently in showers that bring between 60 and 100 inches annually. As a result the Amazon is oppressively humid. Near the ground the air is so saturated that little evaporation is possible. Wet clothes never dry out unless exposed to direct sunlight. If garments are left moist, a mould soon envelops them. Added to these uniformities of temperature and rainfall is the uniformity of time. Like many other tropical forests, the Amazon rain forest is very, very old. Fossil deposits from Trinidad show that the rain-forest plants of 20 million years ago were essentially the same as those growing there now. And forest plants in Indonesia show that the rain forest there has

A tangle of lianas, covered in a damp green stubble of hanging plants, snakes through the dim forest. These tendrils are connecting pipes full of water that is sucked from the ground by the lianas' roots and carried to the forest canopy high above. There, unseen from the forest floor, the lianas' leaves and flowers bloom in the bright tropical sunlight.

existed more or less in its present form for 60 million years. It is reasonable to assume, therefore, that the Amazon forest has been stable for comparable lengths of time.

These many millennia of ever-constant growth conditions have allowed Amazon plants and trees to evolve an extraordinary multiplicity of different species, each one exploiting to the full every niche or job opportunity. The resulting forest is like some ancient civilization that has advanced to a very sophisticated level with a high degree of job specialization and of uniforms. In just one acre of tropical forest, an observer can find perhaps 60 similar looking but different species of tree, in contrast to temperate European woods where he would find only three or four, perhaps less.

The forest is thus a hothouse, a world of no winter, where the life processes can proceed more rapidly than in a cold climate. As a result, plant material is constantly being produced; there is no season when plants cannot germinate, grow, flower and produce fruit.

It is clearly hopeless to attempt an understanding of the Amazon in the terms of European forests, in which differences of soil and climate dictate that species grow some in a stand here, another in a different stand some distance away. In the Amazon, differences are not horizontal but vertical. The rain forest typically contains five layers, ranging from the treetops to the forest floor. The top storey—the fifth—is composed of the widely spaced umbrella-shaped crowns of the tallest trees, usually reaching up to 135 feet. These treetops are fairly open and airy, allowing the light to penetrate to the fourth storey, the mop-shaped, widely spaced crowns of the medium-sized trees. Below them, ranging between 18 and 40 feet, are narrow, closely spaced crowns of the third-storey trees. This layer, which I could see easily from below, is the one that blocks all but a few rays of light from the sparse vegetation of the shrub layer on the ground, and from the few herbs, ferns and saplings of the ground-level first storey.

As I set out to investigate that first layer of jungle, not far from the river I came to two streams. The first I jumped. Across the second lay a fallen tree trunk, and I was tempted to use it as a bridge, but it was covered with moss and looked slippery. I decided I did not want to be seen taking an unexpected plunge by any watching Indian, so I waded through the clear, cold water—the water in these forest streams is always surprisingly cold. Walking on round a fallen tree, which hung in the shrub layer like the mast of a wrecked ship, I saw a beautiful clump of green, white and yellow flowers on one of its upper branches. This burst of colour seemed extremely odd as the tree itself was definitely dead. But as I approached to examine the blossoms they dramatically took flight. They were Phoebis butterflies: some yellow, some white, some green, a variety of colouring that made a marvellous camouflage for the group when it was at rest.

This incident made me realize that I had seen very few flowers in the forest, though occasionally I smelt their odour, sweet and strong. Then I did notice some small white and green-white flowers growing directly from the trunks of trees. I checked with my stick, quite expecting another aerial take-off. But this was a true example of a cauliforous tree, one that produces flowers and fruits directly on its main trunk and larger branches rather than on an intermediary stem.

Evidence of other flowers—small drifts of fallen leaves—lay scattered at my feet. As I looked up to the upper storeys above, I could see them wafting down as a breeze disturbed the canopy. The flowers were not large, as I had expected, but small and white, hardly larger than my finger tip. I had to get used to the Amazon forest dressing itself in such a conservative fashion.

There are, however, several wild exceptions to the Amazon's innate conservatism. Most dramatic are the lianas that writhe upwards vine-like to the light. The lianas are really just trees that do not waste time building their own support to reach the light, but depend on mature trees to give them a helping hand. They writhe up trunks in ribbons, ropes, wires and cables and wind their way onwards across branches to reach enormous lengths—over 600 feet in some cases; such lianas are sometimes thicker than their original support and must entwine themselves around several trees. Often trees collapse under the weight, leaving lianas hanging down from the canopy in great Tarzan-like loops. At last I felt a touch of the exotic.

Lianas have evolved to be as flexible as ropes and cables. Indeed, in the Tupi language they are called *sipos*, or rope-plants. The strands in the main stem are partly, or completely, separated from each other and embedded in softer tissue. They can be twisted or pulled as hard as any hemp rope: the Indians had used some cut lianas to drag the boats up over the rapids. I tried playing Tarzan on a low one, making appropriate whoops. But it is not really possible to make very dramatic displays on these jungle trapezes. Some lianas secrete a violent poison. Others have hooks or claws that scratch abominably. Any would-be Jane would have to be well supplied with sticking plaster.

One species of liana has an unexpected advantage for man: it holds water. I knew how to identify the water-holding liana and managed to find several. To get the water, one must sever the liana in two places. A piece about 18 feet long can hold up to a pint of pure and cool water. Having no machete with me I did not try for a drink. In this region there seemed to be plenty of forest streams, but I imagine that, deep in the interior and in the drier months, to find such pure drinking water might—were it not for the lianas—be a problem.

Lianas are the liberals in a conservative society, ready to adapt to a variety of conditions. They do not need trees to survive: a would-be liana can germinate in open ground and grows into a rather modest, flowering shrub. Abandoned clearings rapidly become overgrown with these liana-shrubs, which constitute a large part of secondary growth forest. Eventually trees seeking light spring up and push through the shrubs. Only then do the lianas grow skyward, seeking light.

The radicals of this conservative forest are the epiphytes or air-plants. They are the most flighty and unconventional of all forms of plant life of the rain forest. They grow upon or actually take root on other trees, shrubs and plants, though they are not usually parasitic. Epiphytes grow at all levels, from the few that enjoy deep shade at ground level to the majority that thrive high up in full daylight. I found a tree with fifteen plants that I could see, and probably this number again were enjoying the high life out of sight.

Though some epiphytes turn stranglers and eventually kill their host, many perform important functions in the forest. One such group are the bromiliads, plants belonging to the pineapple family, which have evolved a fascinating way of conserving water and in doing so become a valuable cog in the forest ecological machine. To guarantee a water supply to last from one rainfall to the next—even in the rain forest there may be three weeks between rainstorms—these plants collect both water and nutrients in tank-like reservoirs. A rosette of narrow leaves on short stems overlap at the base to form a watertight cup, which fills with water, and collects dead leaves, flowers and insects. The dead matter is broken down by micro-organisms into mineral nutrients.

Finding the remains of a bromiliad on a fallen tree and eager for a close up of its reservoir, I peered inside. On the inner surface of the leaves I could see curious little scales. These enable the plants to absorb both water and dissolved nutrients. With their self-contained survival system, epiphytes can take root in most improbable places. In areas where man has built telegraph lines, bromiliads flourish on the wires

Brilliantly coloured, a stemless heisteria flower lights the gloom near the forest floor. This plant, like others in the tropics, ingeniously produces its flowers directly from tree trunks, within easy reach of ground-level pollinators such as ants and slugs. The silvery white fruit (centre) is proof that pollination has taken place.

where their sticky seeds happen to have been deposited by birds.

Here in the forest, one epiphyte had found the slender stem of a dangling liana to be a sufficient foothold. Others were growing on rocks, rooted in small crevices that had trapped dust and moisture. I then came across some thin, red cactus-like leaves adhering to a tree trunk, over-lapping each other like the wrapper of a good cigar. At last I found an example of those most exotic of epiphytes—orchids. Not all orchids live an epiphytic life, but those that do are the classics of their kind. My trophies were two large flowers, one purple and one white. They were the only orchids I came across here, though I was told that a great many had come into bloom several weeks before. I was able to see the way my orchid was able to obtain its water. Free hanging roots were wrapped in a network of dead cells that protect the root from drying out and can absorb the small droplets of moisture like a sponge. The water was stored in the large bulb at the plant's base.

Orchids are so heartachingly beautiful that destructive passions grip some collectors. The number of wild orchids throughout the world—over 15,000 species—is being rapidly reduced by intensive collecting. Hunters even cut down trees in order to obtain plants growing beyond reach. One ardent prospector in Colombia collected 10,000 specimens of the beautiful *Odontoglossum crispum*, by cutting down 4,000 trees, thus destroying the potential source of future orchids.

The area in which I now stood, however, was still untouched but it was also remarkably prim. It reminded me again of a well organized city. Every being was going about its work as though it had been tersely instructed by some sort of civil service memorandum. The work was being done with a frightening attention to economy. This in fact was the secret of the clean forest. Leaves and flowers from above were con-stantly falling and constantly being cleared away. The mechanism of forest growth in the Amazon was clearly utterly different from anything I had experienced before.

In a northern temperate forest, where the main leaf fall is, of course, in the autumn, the leaves are slowly broken down by minute organisms to form humus, the vegetable matter of the soil. The deciduous trees then reabsorb the minerals from the soil through their roots and recycle them into the plant system.

But in the Amazon forest the soils are leached of most minerals, bacteria and other organisms. Anything that is broken down is carried away by the frequent rains and river floods. No rich soil, few bacteria, no minerals: how on earth does the luxuriant forest survive?

The answer lies principally in the mass of fungi that coat the trees. Particularly vital are the fungi that live in close association with the smaller roots of the trees and other plants. They cover the fine rootlets with a whitish felt and even penetrate between the plant cells. These associations of roots and fungi, called mycorrhiza, are at least one key to the trees' nutrition, though in such a complex system there are obviously others. They are able to transfer the mineral nutrients from the decaying leaves and wood that land on them directly to the living roots. As a result only a very small fraction of the soluble mineral matter is ever allowed to reach the soil. Perhaps here was a further clue to the existence of buttresses: could they be a method of exposing a greater area of tree to the life-giving fungi?

Fungi do not provide all the answers of course: the insects—especially ants—on the forest floor and on the plants play an important role too, as do bacteria and worms. But I was, at least, aware of the basic mechanisms of forest life: the whole cycle of nutrients is short-circuited. The forest does not exist *in* the soil so much as *above* it.

I realized that many of my observations during my time in the region had helped me to see exactly how this principle was being carried out. I remembered the informal toilet that had been set up not far from the camp. Here in the humid, warm tropical conditions, the fungi had been at work and disposed of the faeces.

The ants, I could see, had an important role to play. One file of ants, each carrying a nearly circular piece of leaf, I recognized as the Sauva. Henry Walter Bates had mentioned them in his book on the Amazon, but he did not know exactly what they were doing with those bits of leaf. With the advantage of time, I did know. I crawled along after the insects on my hands and knees until they reached their nest. The workers struggled down the hole, each clutching his leaf. If an ant got stuck with his burden, he would tussle with it, with a kind of desperate patience, while the others passed him by.

In galleries below ground these insects deposit the leaf-material and then cultivate a kind of mould on it, which they feed to their young. The leaves are thereby destroyed and turned into inorganic material which can be quickly assimilated by the vegetation overhead. Clearly, the ants had their instructions, as did the termites, the moulds, the fungi, the parasites, and the parasites growing on parasites, and (for they exist) the parasites growing on parasites growing on parasites.

Thousands of species of plants and animals and micro-organisms were filling every single niche of the forest, catching up the dying life practically as it fell—often before it fell—and throwing it back into the air, back to the real surface of the forest in the canopy far above.

I had been staring into the ant-hill for five or ten minutes when I heard a crashing noise in the forest. Generally speaking, there is relatively little risk from wild animals in the Amazon. Nevertheless, down on my hands and knees, I did not feel general, I felt particular, and I was aware of a certain prickling at the back of my neck. It was no comfort to remember, either, that if I had been up and walking about I probably would have been making so much noise that any animal would have run away. The fact was that I had not been making noise and something—something big—was coming my way. I was chivalrously armed with a stick, a pen-knife and a couple of orchids.

I stood up, and through the trees about 40 or 50 feet away caught sight of a large shape, that seemed to be accompanied by a smaller shape. The large animal had a head that was oddly curved into a snout. It was about the size of a pony, and was apparently browsing. The animals were tapirs, which I had longed to see. But old habits die slowly, and the instant I recognized them I made an automatic gesture of recognition. As if signalling to someone in a library I politely cleared my throat. I could have cut it a moment later.

The large tapir looked up. It had probably never heard a human throat cleared before, and it certainly did not like the sound. It bolted straight through the forest, diagonally away from me, the baby tapir following. In a moment it was gone and I could only hear it crashing through the trees off to my left. I was heart-broken, and humiliated. Very soon, I felt, the librarian would come up to me and suggest that I leave the reading room and come back another day when my catarrh had cleared up. On the whole, it was an inept performance. On the other hand, I was pretty sure that if I had been looking for a tapir I never would have found one. There is something to be said for blundering, but not much.

Hidden Beauties of the Rain Forest

To a casual visitor, the twilit interior of the Amazon forest, darkened by the thick canopy of the tree-tops, often appears sombre or boring. Even botanists have been surprised that no profusion of brilliant tropical blossoms can be seen by a man walking in the forest. Only a few flowers grow in the thin, light-starved soil beneath the canopy, and they are small and pale.

The real beauty of the forest is found elsewhere. High up in the sunlit treetop canopy, orchids and other flowering plants grow from the branches. They have aerial roots and are called epiphytes by botanists and "daughters of the air" by the Indians. From this aerial garden fragrant, pungent and narcotic smells waft down to the hot, humid air below. In forest clearings, away from the darkness, an occasional bright red passion flower ornaments the foliage like some exotic butterfly. And in still river lakes, water hyacinths and tropical lilies create patterns of pink, purple and white.

As the explorer becomes accustomed to the forest, even the gloomy green interior takes on a certain beauty. Climbing plants like peperomia decorate the tree trunks with leaf mosaics; and lianas, or rope plants, using mature trees for support, writhe upwards to the light or hang down in gigantic green coils and loops.

The forest is full of botanical oddities like the Cannon-Ball Tree, whose fruit are as hard as iron and fall to the ground with a loud crash, and the Victoria Amazonica lily, whose huge leaves, veined like steel girders, inspired the framework of Joseph Paxton's monumental glass hall, the Crystal Palace, built for London's Great Exhibition in 1851.

Numerous other plants have proved valuable or even essential to forest life: food plants, such as the avocado, grow wild; other species provide poisons with which Indians tip hunting spears and make drugs to combat disease and provide an escape into hallucinations. Still other plants—notably the fungi—are vital to the forest life-cycle. They appear merely picturesque, but without them the forest could not live. They decompose forest detritus and return it to the trees and plants as nourishment, creating a functional cycle of perfect economy and sustaining the beauty that waits in the Amazon for those who know where to look.

In the sombre gloom of the Amazon forest, a decorative peperomia drapes a naked tree-trunk. Its variegated green and white leaves, which have won it popularity as a house plant in Europe, sometimes creep up from beds of moss at the base of tree-trunks but may also hang down in swathes from root-holds in the branches overhead.

THE HUGE LEAVES OF A VICTORIA AMAZONICA LILY

A BLUSHING CRINUM LILY

A BLOOD-RED PASSION FLOWER

FLOWERS OF A POISONOUS NIGHTSHADE

A HAIRY COOKEIANA TRICHOLOMA FUNGUS

AN EARTH STAR FUNGUS OPEN, EXPOSING ITS SPORE HOLE

MARASMIUS MUSHROOMS SPROUTING FROM THE FUNGUS'S WEB-LIKE MAIN BODY

AN AVOCADO PEAR

THE HARD FRUIT OF A CANNON-BALL TREE

4/ A Jungle Bestiary

In the jungle, vegetable nature and animal nature struggled for survival. Enormous caterpillars savaged the leaves, and birds savaged the caterpillars. H. M. TOMLINSON/THE SEA AND THE JUNGLE

As soon as I reached the Amazon I found that it is far from the open zoo of popular imagination. The animals are there, somewhere, but a few hours' personal experience are enough to show that here the insects rule —and that insects are no friends of man. I stayed for few days in a tiny riverside settlement on the river Jari. It had a dock, a general store, and about 25 houses, though most of these were little more than shacks. Nevertheless, there were probably more than 100 people here, and for the 20 or 30 others who lived even further up the river it was civilization. As usual in such places in Brazil, the quality, if not the quantity, of the hospitality was superb. I had the best room in town, and the luxury of this was hardly dimmed by the fact that it was just that— a room and nothing else. It had hooks on the walls, however, to string a hammock; in these settlements, most rooms are built to exactly hammock-size. And it was clean. In the tiny kitchen a woman was apologetically cooking what turned out to be just about the best fish I have ever eaten. I even had a beer. But then came the mutúca flies.

There are a number of species of this fly, some large, some small, keeping to the sunlight or the shade according to their natures. This particular species was about the size of a housefly and hovered just inside the window of the room where there was sunlight, making forays into the shade as well. I had never seen them in a house before, and as we were so close to the forest their presence here might have been temporary. They are lethargic creatures, like sand-flies, but their bite is extremely painful. They do not seem to be bothered that they might be killed by you—just as long as they get their lances in first. Their effect is cumulative: one bite is annoying, five are excruciating, ten are maddening, and more than twenty makes one uncertain of, and almost indifferent to, survival.

In this village there were mutúca flies, mosquitoes, pium flies, not to mention the spiders, ticks, fleas (including the jigger flea, a tiny red creature in the underbrush that burrows into one's skin) and centipedes. There were also flies in the region that deposit their larvae in scratches and wounds, producing ulcers, and one delightful fly that, with the active aid of a mosquito, transfers its eggs to humans in such a way that they can slip into punctures in the skin and there grow into maggots. However much one may love nature, circumstances like this check Arcadian romanticism; it can return again when one is safely sheltered under an ecologically indefensible cloud of DDT.

When I tried to think of all the animals I wanted to see, however, those old traveller's tales kept flooding into my thoughts, the tales of the Green Hell, of weird, wonderful and dangerous creatures everywhere in the forest. Jaguars crouching behind tree buttresses, boas draping from the trees, anacondas lurking by the rivers, alligators waiting on the banks. But of course the forest is not like this. In the forests most animals are small—the problem of moving through the trees when danger threatens has prevented any really large animals surviving for long inside the forest proper, particularly anywhere far from water. And most are highly camouflaged, which creates a problem of its own; how does each recognize his mate? To move around in daytime would make the camouflage useless, so most forest animals stay motionless during the day and move about only at dusk or later. Then it is more difficult to be seen, of course, but they can be heard. This is why the forest is so hushed by day but noisy with recognition signals—bird calls and chatterings of monkeys, for example—at night.

On my first afternoon I took a walk out of this settlement back through the forest, and along an overgrown trail, which would eventually return to the river. Even though I knew that I would probably see very few animals in the daytime, and hear only the odd screech or call, I felt apprehensive knowing that animals *were* there, lurking somewhere, hidden so well even from their own kind. I stared hard at the leaves hoping to recognize an insect such as a katydid, pretending to be a leaf—but they were all leaves. Tree bark turned out to be tree bark and not a cryptically coloured moth; twigs were twigs and not motionless praying mantids.

I reached a fork in the path, and as the way to the right seemed to move towards higher forest I followed it. I was not far from a stream, and knowing that there was more likelihood of seeing animals a bit larger than insects the closer to the water I got, I trod slowly and carefully and stared intently into the dark middle distance. My intentness was rewarded, but only for a second. Something about 18 inches long darted out from the right and raced ahead of me into the dark forest. It was a rodent, a paca, unmistakeable with its brown flanks spotted with white. I must have walked too close to its daytime hideout and frightened the creature. Pacas are right to be fearful of man, for their meat is very tasty and they are hunted by the Indians for food.

I looked around me, and saw hundreds of trees, a few of the many millions in the forest. I had seen just one paca, one of a local population that must have run into hundreds. That, I thought, would be that for the rest of the walk. The chances of seeing anything larger—another tapir for instance—were exceedingly slim. The reason for this lies in the extraordinary adaptations all creatures have been forced to evolve to survive in this waterlogged forest. The first time you encounter the forest animals, however much you have read about them, you are struck by their strangeness, and you are fascinated by the many devices they have evolved over 70 million years of isolation to enable them to climb, cling, float or swim, and the equally intriguing ways in which they have overcome the problems of feeding and breeding.

What would be simple ground beetles in other parts of the world here have comb-toothed claws to cling to tree leaves, since the heavy rains and flooding demand a means of escape upwards into the trees. Birds whose Old World relations spend a lot of time on the ground in the Amazon are adapted to perching and have long curved claws to ensure a solid grip on the branches. Frogs which in other lands hatch out as tadpoles in ponds or streams find no such relatively still waters in the Amazon basin (only torrential flows that would carry the eggs into the jaws of countless predators) and instead lay their eggs in the bromiliad flower's "water-tanks". Or carry their eggs in safety on their backs until they metamorphose into little frogs. Here there is the only fully aquatic marsupial in the world—the yapok or water opossum, with webbed feet for swimming (the female's pouch somehow protects her young as she swims and dives). Mammals such as pigs and rodents are as much at home in water as they are on land, and even the sluggish sloth

Almost perfectly camouflaged, a brown moth rests against the bark of a tree. Only its fore-limbs (left) and the serrated edges of its fore-wings (right) are discernible. In the centre, dark patches on the wings merge almost precisely into a ring of ageing bark.

swims pretty well when it isn't hanging upside down in a tree.

Then, of course, there are the monkeys, which seem to be more at home in the trees than monkeys anywhere else—indeed many never come down to the ground at all. They are vastly different from Old World monkeys—one would have to go back 60 or 70 million years to find a common ancestor—and some have developed an amazingly useful fifth limb, a prehensile tail. On the underside of the tail is a patch of sensitive skin, like the palm of the hand, which turns these animals into the super-acrobats of the trees. Monkeys are not the only creatures with prehensile tails in the Amazon. Anteaters, kinkajous (a sort of racoon), porcupines, opossums: nowhere else on earth are there so many mammals with grasping tails. This diversity extends to any creature—especially birds—that can escape the forest floor. The upper canopy is an ornithologist's paradise. It contains almost half the world total of 8,600 species—and doubtless there are a myriad of species still to be discovered. There are 319 sorts of hummingbird alone (North America has only 18).

The reason for the diversity of the fauna can be explained simply. The huge variety of plant life gives an unrivalled range of different foods. Without too much competition each species can evolve its own place in the great forest, and over the years refine its habits to fit a particular ecological niche, some amazingly specialized. There is no limitation here: in the Amazon's stable, equable climate, no animal has to face up to seasonal hazards and each has a much better chance of survival than it would anywhere else.

There is one major problem: food. Since the immense variety of plant life leads to a wide scattering of any one plant species, an animal adapted to eat that plant has a real struggle to find its food. It has to range as widely as the plant it eats. It is for this reason that the forest is so empty of creatures, especially on the lower levels.

The only creatures which do gather in great numbers are the insects. The long history of the forest has enabled countless butterflies, moths, ants, termites, wasps and bees to evolve and stay there. South America has more species of butterfly than any other continental area, even while thousands of species are still to be identified. Some are brightly and boldly coloured, warning predators of an unpalatable taste; others mimic distasteful butterflies, tricking predators to disdain them; others have jagged colouring to break up their body outline, making them difficult to spot in the forest; others have startling eye-spots on their wings to frighten predators. The variations are innumerable.

There are so many mosquitoes in the Amazon that little is known about even those 218 species that have been classified and there are probably hundreds of unidentified species, about which nothing is known. Having spent considerable time in mosquito lands in the last 20 years, I was used to mosquitoes mounting their virulent attacks at night. But in the Amazon riverland they are active day and night. The only defence for bald people like myself is a plastic showercap.

At my feet paraded the ants, which with their burdens of leaves were destroying and recycling the forest nutrients. Their variety rivals that of other creatures. There is a kind of fire-ant usually found on open ground and often near settlements which will consume every bit of food not hung up with cords soaked with insect repellent; it will even eat starch from clothing. Its sting is intolerable, and people often pack up and leave until the invasion passes. The ants that eat only vegetation do even more damage. Leaf-cutting saubas can destroy a garden or plantation overnight. They seem to do less damage in the forest because their favourite trees are more widely spread out.

Then there are the columns of carnivorous army ants, marching through the forest, producing a faint hissing sound as they search behind every leaf and twig for food. They can turn the cadaver of a small animal into a skeleton within a few minutes. Henry Walter Bates, the English naturalist, describes the movements of one species of these army ants, called Taocas. "Wherever they move, the whole animal world is set in commotion, and every creature tries to get out of their way." I considered: millions of leaves feed millions of ants: millions of ants feed . . . anteaters. Ant-eating ants, ant-eating frogs, ant-eating birds, ant-eating mammals—ants and myriads of other protein rich insects provide food for as wide an assortment of creatures as you could hope to find anywhere.

The true anteaters themselves—the giant anteater, and its closest relations—are purists, and subsist on a diet of only ants and termites, plus of course a few unavoidable bits of dirt. The giant anteater is one of the largest animals of the Amazon, up to $5\frac{1}{2}$ feet long including an enormous bushy tail that sweeps the ground as the animal moves. Its long tapering snout contains an even longer, extensile tongue covered with a sticky saliva to pick up the ants. The ant hills and termite mounds are dug up with huge claws, claws so large, especially on the front feet, that the anteater has to walk on the outside of its hands and feet, giving it an awkward gait. The giant anteater stays on the ground—although it can, of course, swim—but the other smaller ant-eaters live mostly in the lower layers of the forest canopy, and dig out the arboreal ants and termites.

It is in the forest canopy that the true wealth of Amazonian animals is to be found. Here live honeycreepers, pigeons, marmosets, coatis, cotingas, macaws, monkeys, hummingbirds—all rarely seen from the forest floor because of the denseness of the leafy roof above. I would have liked to explore the canopy, but to get there you must contend with biting ants, thorny lianas and rotten branches. Here live the toucans, huge and gaudy with an outsized bill which looks heavy, but is in fact a honeycomb affair and therefore quite light. No one seems to know its exact function. Some have described it as a useful device for snatching fruits, others as an instrument of ornamentation or advertisement. Here, too, is the huge but agile harpy eagle.

Above the whole forest soar the vultures, the carrion eaters. If the vultures do not tidy off the loose ends in the intertangled web of life and death, the process starts again from where we started, with the carrion-eating insects on the forest floor.

I shortly came upon a stream, which obviously drained into the Jari further on. The stream was only about a foot and a half deep, with a relatively clean, sandy bottom. As there was a great deal of underbrush on either side, I decided to walk straight down the centre of the stream. I was wearing heavy duty tennis shoes which are ideal for the jungle because they can be dried out so quickly. Those glorious mosquito-boots they try to sell you in the big cities of Brazil look romantic—like ten-gallon hats look in the American West—but they are not very practical.

Struggling down the stream with my trousers rolled up, I noticed off to one side a tall tree with large, deeply indented leaves. It was a Cecropia, or Imbauba as it is called in Brazil. I had seen these on the banks of many Amazon rivers, and I always looked at them closely because their leaves are favoured by the sloths. There are two species of sloth, one with two clawed toes on its front legs, and the other with three, and the three-toed sloth is particularly fond of the Imbauba. I was dying to see one of these weird creatures.

The trouble is that sloths are just as anxious not to be seen, and they are so well adapted to trees that they are practically vegetative. Much of the time they are resting, motionless, hanging upside down from the branches, but even when they are moving, their progress is very slow. They are hard to notice because they look just like a bunch of leaves.

Although most Amazonian birds spend
their lives in the forest canopy, a few
species—some of which are illustrated
here—stay close to the river banks,
living on the specialized diets available
there. Many of them are fish eaters.
The egret and ibis, for example, wade
in shallow waters, hunting fish near
the surface with their sharp beaks.
The black cormorant hunts in deeper
water, diving down and snatching its
prey from beneath the surface with its
hooked beak. Other birds feed from
the banks, among them the insect-eating
red-headed blackbird. The most
curious of these riverside birds is the
primitive hoatzin. With wing muscles
so weak that it can fly barely 100 yards
before becoming exhausted, it leads an
almost sedentary existence close to its
favourite food source of arum leaves.

HOATZINS

RED-HEADED BLACKBIRD

COMMON EGRET

NEOTROPIC CORMORANTS

SCARLET IBISES AND SPOONBILLS

Their fur (which grows in the opposite direction from that of other mammals—from stomach to back to enable rain to fall off) is brownish, but in the rainy season takes on a greenish hue, due to microscopic green algae which live in grooves in the fur. In addition small green moths can often be seen crawling through the sloth's hair, probably feeding on the algae—a very odd example of co-operative existence. The sloth would appear to need this elaborate form of camouflage to protect it from predators since it is so slow-moving and slow-witted, but it is not actually defenceless. With its back against a branch it can swipe out viciously with its hooked forelegs, and do quite a bit of damage to an attacker.

I climbed out of the stream and stared up, hoping to see the smiling baby-face of the sloth amongst the Cecropia leaves. I had a stick with me and I thought that the animal, if it was there, might move if I hit the tree. I drew back to give myself room for the blow and struck. As I did so I dimly remembered something else I had heard about the Cecropia and tried to stop myself. It was too late—ants were crawling all over me and several of them stung like wasps. They were extremely painful and I dived for the water before any more of them could get inside my clothes: I had to tear off my clothes to rid myself of the creatures.

I looked back at the tree, now remembering exactly what I had heard —that the Cecropia tree is the home of one of the Amazonian fire-ants. The Cecropia is hollow and the fire-ant has a ready-made nest inside. I do not know if the sloth is ever bothered by the ants—perhaps it moves so slowly in order not to attract their attention. All in all the interaction of animal and vegetable life in this one tree is quite bewildering. It must surely have taken aeons to set up this delicate balance of life.

At last I came close to the river. The stream widened and became so choked with underbrush that it was impossible to go farther; but I could see light ahead and could hear the water tearing at the riverside vegetation. I was sopping wet and tired, and even looking forward to the mutúcas back in the settlement, and perhaps another bottle of beer. Nevertheless I could hardly say that the afternoon had been strenuous, and I had been in no particular danger.

Looking down into the water I saw what appeared to be a large snake and I scrambled towards the crumbling bank of the stream and clawed my way up the matted roots. Then I looked back, expecting a giant anaconda, the sucuri, to be following me, intent on swallowing me alive. Big snakes have always made me feel a bit queasy.

The creature was moving sluggishly, and I noted that it was only about six feet long, and not two or three times that size, as I had imagined. It was not even a snake, but a sort of eel. I sighed with relief, realizing how ridiculous all this was. In fact, if it had been an anaconda, one of this size would have done very little damage even if it had wished. Anacondas are not poisonous, and unless extremely hungry or provoked, they rarely attack people. They do grow, of course, into the largest of the living snakes—the longest ever measured was 37 feet 6 inches—and they are capable of swallowing animals weighing 150 pounds. Anacondas haunt the dark pools of the swamps and tributaries and prey on the alligator-like caimans. Other more usual prey are water birds, and the capybaras, which are plentiful and easy to catch. In killing its prey the anaconda wraps its body around its victim and suffocates it, then proceeds to swallow it whole.

The eel on the other hand, was almost certainly an electric one, and had I touched it I would have had quite a shock—the equivalent of putting a wet finger for a moment in a 220-volt socket. They use their electric sense for navigation (their vision is poor) and to locate and stun prey. The fish does not kill anything the size of a man for food, of course, but there have been cases of men losing consciousness from its shock, and then drowning.

The electric current is generated in the muscle system of the body. Alexander von Humboldt, the German naturalist, was the first scientist to describe the creature, not many years after Galvani and Volta made their first experiments with electricity. Humboldt wrote of accidentally stepping on one: "I do not remember of having ever received from the discharge of a large Leyden jar a more dreadful shock than that which I experienced. I was affected during the rest of the day with a violent pain in the knees and in almost every joint." I watched the eel for a while, from a discreet distance, then I went back to the settlement.

So far I had seen at close quarters only the animal life of the forest. A few days later I began a trip in a motor launch eastwards down the river from Manáus and into a *várzea* lake, the Lago dos Reis, to see life in the water. From Manáus downstream, the Amazon becomes really much more of a sea than a river. Fresh-water dolphins arch above the waves and fishing-birds circle overhead. It is at once apparent that these turbid waters harbour much more life than the clear black ones of the river Negro. Over 700 different kinds of fish have been noted within a 20 mile radius of Manáus, which is nearly as many species as in all the fresh waters of North America. On one estimate there could be 2,000 different fish species in the Amazon basin. Standing on the deck of the launch, I asked the captain if he had ever eaten dolphin meat. He shook his head and turned nervously away, embarrassed. A dolphin's flesh is perfectly edible but many men here fear it will make them impotent.

Unfortunately myths have not protected other animals here. The sea-cow or manatee is now growing very rare, which is a great pity, for the mammal is harmless. It is enormous; the adults are over two yards long and measure nearly a yard and a half across the thickest part of their fat cigar-shaped bodies.

The habit which the mother manatee has, of clasping her suckling to her breast with flippers, sometimes making doleful, sighing noises, is probably responsible for the legend of mermaids out at sea. The sailors were a long way from land after all, and prone to wishful thinking. Such legends have never arisen in the Amazon because the creature is remarkably hideous at close quarters, with a mouth deprived of all but molar teeth, and an upper cleft so that it can shovel in river plants. The fat of this timid vegetarian yields large quantities of oil for cooking and lighting, and its tough hide has been used by the Indians for making shields, and by the Europeans for making engine-belts. Accordingly, men have hunted the manatee without quarter and it has been disappearing in spite of there being almost unlimited amounts of food for it in the Amazon rivers.

Its feeding habits could in fact make it much more valuable alive than dead. It lives on water plants, the high grass known as *canarana*, which often chokes *várzea* lakes, sometimes to such an extent that it is impossible for boats to fight their way through to clear water. More significantly for the future, it thrives on the insidious water hyacinth which has recently begun to invade the Amazon. The river is so huge that the plant causes very little inconvenience now, but if experience on other great rivers of the world can be any guide, this stubborn water plant could cause trouble one day. Already both the Nile and the Congo are choked with it in some areas. The plant has blocked shipping, irrigation canals and drainage ditches; and it has menaced almost every hydro-electric project built in the tropics since the end of the Second World War. Millions of pounds are spent on herbicides every year to combat it, but with very little success. The manatee is one of the few creatures on earth which will clear the waterways for nothing; moreover, if manatees were well husbanded, they would produce meat from what they eat. If this entirely beneficial, peaceful, beautiful, ugly animal ever does become extinct on the Amazon the men living here are going

Among the most abundant and therefore the most preyed upon species in the sparsely populated Amazon forests are the frogs. In order to survive, they have evolved a great variety of defences. Tree frogs have friction pads on their toes for quick escape, and the arrow-poison frogs display garish colours to advertise possession of some of the world's deadliest toxins. The variegated toad camouflages itself on the shadowy forest floor, and the bulky marine toad inflates itself in the gullet of any predator too hungry or inexperienced to heed the poison in its skin glands.

RED TREE FROG

VARIEGATED TOAD

ARROW-POISON FROG

THREE-STRIPED ARROW-POISON FROG

MARINE TOAD

to regret it bitterly. Conservationists are often accused of being too shrill but here, at least, the louder the cries of alarm the better.

As it turned out, when we turned into the Lago dos Reis our passage into the central portion was eventually blocked by heavy mats of water grasses and other plants that filled the channel heading from the river. We travelled for some miles into this drowned world, where it was impossible to tell where the land began and the water stopped—if indeed nature had ever intended the two to be divided.

As we ploughed through the floating plant-cover it closed behind us like a viscous pudding. In some places it was almost solid enough to walk on and great rafts of it rocked on our approach. All life down here seems to be adapted for this half-solid world. There are tiny flying fish, and even a species of lizard that literally walks on the water for a few yards. It is called a basilisk and is usually quadrupedal, but when alarmed it runs on two back legs, its long toes allowing it to skim over water at speed (in Spanish it is called Jesu Cristo because of this ability), until it sinks down and swims away.

After some hours of ripping through thickening vegetation, we stripped a gear in one of our motors and had to turn back. It was a very tricky operation and, in spite of constant counsel from some rowdy capuchins, we did not get back to the river until nightfall.

The next morning we rented two dugout canoes to explore the flooded forest. My own canoe was captained and crewed by a half-Indian man and his young daughter. I was bailing wildly and thinking of the reptiles slithering below, while the Brazilian maintained a superb aplomb. My friend practised bird-calls when he was not, with deft flicks of his paddle, guiding us beyond reach of protruding branches and lianas. His daughter languidly picked up a gourd from time to time to scoop up some of the water. "You'll find a jiboa here, if you find it anywhere," my friend said when we landed, picking up his gun and leading the way into the forest. A jiboa is a boa constrictor, an entirely harmless snake to man which grows to 15 feet in length. It is so harmless that people frequently catch boas young and use them in their houses to dispose of rats and mice and even bats; though as house pets they become less desirable after they are a few yards long. I was determined to see one big snake at least, and not in a house if I could help it.

My friend enjoyed hunting; he had intended to come up here for some weeks past, and I asked to join him, though I do not shoot. The last time he had come this way he had seen several jiboas.

We had been walking for about an hour, crossing small streams on the way, all of which were flowing not towards the river, but westward, probably towards a small tributary not far away. The jiboa lives on land, feeding on small animals, but I believe it is also at home in the water and does not wander too far from it. Here the underbrush was rather heavy; in several places I could see that large trees had been felled. At last, breathless, I stopped by a fallen tree trunk and sat down, leaving my companion to go on alone. Suddenly, I heard a shot.

I stood up looking for my friend. A few minutes later I heard a kind of tumult in the leaves, almost like rain. I stood perfectly still and searched for the source of the sound as it came closer. Then I saw a snake. It was unlike anything I had imagined it would be; it was not sinuous, but rather seemed to be flowing, like sun-dappled water. When it met obstructions it passed over or around them with an uninterrupted, purposeful motion.

Surprisingly I was not alarmed. The creature's movements were peculiarly lyrical. It came down the rise ahead of me, and then flowed wonderfully off to my left and disappeared in the underbrush. Possibly the fact that it was quite large—between nine and twelve feet—made it less menacing. That may not sound logical. But it was simply a great, dumb, beautiful creature which was terrified and I could understand that perfectly.

My friend came down a few minutes later, and I realized that he had not seen the snake at all. He had been firing at something else, his shot had gone wild and he suggested that we go on, since any game in this part of the forest would have been frightened away.

We wandered around for a few more hours without success. I never did tell him about the snake: firstly because I thought that he might insist on going after it, and later because I was ashamed of deceiving him. But I knew that I would never be afraid of large snakes again.

As we wandered back through the quiet, dark world, I felt strangely uneasy. The unhappy affair with the snake had made me realize that modern civilized man is the one species that the forest has not managed to absorb and mould to its ways.

The Singular Creatures

Large animals are astonishingly rare in the Amazon. They are scattered so sparsely that the early European explorers, hoping to live by hunting, nearly starved. One, reduced to eating a valued specimen of spider monkey, lamented: "Nothing but the hardest necessity could have driven me so near to cannibalism." The reason for the scarcity of animals is simply the dearth of food to support them: the forest floor, dark and barren beneath the soaring tree canopy, grows too few plants to support many herbivores, and where herbivores are lacking, so are carnivores.

Those animals that have prospered survive only because they have adopted strange shapes and behaviour patterns, to cope with the peculiar conditions of Amazonian rivers and forests. Many animals climb high in the rain forest canopy or swim along the waterlogged river banks where light and food are concentrated. The alligator or caiman (right) lives in the river but feeds on its banks. Even the sloth, a cumbersome mammal which year after year may hang upside-down in the same tree, can swim when the need arises.

Like the sloth, many of the monkeys are so well adapted to tree-living that they rarely come down to earth. Small and evolutionarily far distant from their Old World counterparts, many have prehensile tails to enhance their mobility and make it easier for them to stake out large arboreal territories, which they guard jealously. The tiny douroucouli monkey boxes intruders with its hands while the howler monkey loudly berates any unwelcome competitor.

Some of the water-adapted animals seem outrageous to European eyes. The plant-eating tapir, for example, is an ungainly mixture of rhinoceros and horse, with a highly mobile two-inch trunk that it uses to search for food along the riverbanks. The capybara, another bank dweller, is a rodent the size of a pig, while the manatee, a large, hairless water mammal, must rank as one of the world's ugliest and at the same time, friendliest beasts. It frequently forms attachments for boats, following them for long periods.

More familiar animals, like the deer and puma, are recent immigrants that settled in the river forest only after a land link with North America was formed three million years ago.

The scales of the black caiman, the largest alligator in the Amazon, take on the blue-green colour of the water it slithers through. Such camouflage, and even the ability to breathe submerged, through raised nostrils, have not saved the caiman from ruthless slaughter both by hide exporters and by Indians who fear its vicious teeth.

Its bushy tail spread out behind, a giant anteater launches itself into water.

A ponderous manatee uses its paddle-like limbs to manoeuvre itself under water.

Adaptable Mammals in a Watery World

Most Amazonian mammals—even when basically land creatures—are adapted to this world of rivers and flood-plains. The giant anteater prefers the high ground that harbours the ants and termites on which it feeds. With the long claws on its forepaws and its extraordinary, sabre-like snout, it delves through the tough walls of the nests and drags out the insects with its ten-inch, sticky tongue. Yet in times of flood it can use its powerful front limbs to propel itself through the water.

The tapir, a smaller but nonetheless hefty relative of the rhinoceros, is rarely far from water to which it rushes precipitously at the first sign of danger. It is generally to be found wallowing up to its knees and browsing placidly on the vegetation, but it can also swim strongly when the need arises.

Water is the permanent habitat of the grotesque manatee, also known as the sea-cow because of the way the female suckles its young. Normally an estuary creature adapted to sea water, the manatee has strayed up many of the Amazon tributaries. It feeds on vegetation under water, tearing it away from the river bed with a powerful, prehensile upper lip. Otherwise it may float contentedly near the surface with its back arched, or even "stand" vertically in the shallows, resting on its tail, with only its head protruding.

A tapir peers at the intruding photographer from the safety of the river, its small trunk briefly stilled from its constant search for food.

Secured by its long prehensile tail, a woolly monkey hangs contentedly in a palm tree.

Agility and Immobility in the Tree Canopy

The monkeys and the sloths are superbly suited to the Amazon forest—they rarely descend from the trees—yet in the solutions both kinds of animals have evolved to arboreal life, they are utter opposites. All Amazon monkeys are nimble acrobats while the slow motion of the sloths explains the connotation their name has acquired.

One small simian, the woolly monkey, moves high in the crowns of trees where much of Amazon life takes place. Its agility is enhanced by a prehensile tail by which it can swing from branch to branch. The tail is, in effect, a fifth limb. The underside of the tip is hairless and the skin is ridged like that of the hands and feet.

Sloths are found in two distinct types, either two-toed or three-toed. Sluggish and slow-witted, they may spend years almost motionless in a single tree, suspended upside down by long, hooklike claws. These are so effectively adapted to hanging that walking is almost impossible: on the rare occasions that the sloths descend to ground level they can move only by heaving themselves along on their bellies.

But the sloth is not so vulnerable to predators as it might appear. Green algae in its coat provide a camouflage, blending with the surrounding vegetation, and its upside-down existence is protection in itself: the large cats tend to topple over in their efforts to reach it.

The sloth's hair grows down from the belly, an adaptation which allows rain to run off freely in the animal's upside-down position.

Mother and infant douroucoulis peer gingerly through dense vegetation. The only nocturnal monkeys of the Amazon forest, they sleep by day in hollow tree trunks, emerging at dusk to eat fruit and hunt insects with the aid of enlarged, owl-like eyes.

A howler monkey warns intruders to keep out of its territory with a howl that can be heard three miles away. The sound, which reverberates around the forest each day at dawn, is produced in an enlarged voice box. It also serves to call others of the band to feed.

A female swamp deer raises its head from its refuge in a dark tangle of vegetation.

Hunter and Hunted on the Jungle Fringe

The puma and its prey, the swamp deer, are among the Amazon region's minority of land creatures. Lacking refined adaptations to an arboreal or river existence, they are scattered in the region's higher fringes where the darkened river-forest hesitantly gives way to grassy savannah.

The puma eats more swamp deer than anything else, but it also preys on smaller mammals such as monkeys and birds. The puma exerts its superiority by sheer strength. About the size of a leopard, but with the uniform colouring of a lion, it can cover 20 feet in one bound and leap skywards to a height of 15 feet. It can climb, but unlike a fellow carnivore in the Amazon, the jaguar, it rarely does so.

After stealthily tracking a deer or monkey, it hurls itself on to the animal's back and bites swiftly through its throat.

The swamp deer defends itself by timidly hiding in dense vegetation for most of the day. In swampy areas, a tough membrane stretched between the toes of each hoof helps prevent it sinking into the soft ground. Only under the protective covering of darkness does it emerge, warily, into riverside clearings to feed on grass, reeds and aquatic plants.

Although not a strong swimmer, the swamp deer will sometimes retreat into the water when hard pressed by a predator.

A puma pauses expectantly in its search for prey. The sleek carnivore rarely attacks man, but feeds on deer, monkeys and birds.

Capybaras look up apprehensively as they browse with their young along a marshy riverbank. Their pig-like appearance is deceptive for, although they grow to a length of four feet and a weight of 160 pounds, they are not pigs but rodents—the world's largest. They congregate in groups of up to 20, feeding on grasses and aquatic plants. Using webbed feet, they swim strongly and to escape predators may submerge completely for up to ten minutes.

5/ The Scholarly Explorers

There have been few such noble labourers in the cause of
Natural Science.

CHARLES DARWIN OF ALFRED RUSSEL WALLACE/LETTER, 1859

In the great age of exploration in the 18th and 19th Centuries, the Amazon wilderness and the interior of Africa were both intensively explored by white men. But the manner of their exploration could hardly have been more different. The mysteries of the Dark Continent were unlocked by well-to-do gentlemen adventurers, who marched at the head of large expeditions financed by learned societies, governments or even newspapers and won great popular acclaim for being the first to penetrate the unknown. We see them still as they were seen then, poised heroically between the indestructible covers of Victorian books, clear-eyed and courageous. But the men who penetrated the even less hospitable Amazon forests were scholars, many of them penniless, and they had no large expeditions to march at the head of. They were explorer-scientists, magnetized, not by ambition or hunger for adventure, but by an overriding desire to discover the laws of nature. A few, like the Frenchman, Charles Marie de la Condamine, and the German, Alexander von Humboldt, were wealthy aristocrats as well as scientists. Many were rather nondescript, single-minded scholars, such as one might meet in any university common room. Among them were shy and peculiar men such as the Englishman, Alfred Russel Wallace, who, from his researches in the Amazon, conceived the principles of evolution at exactly the same time as Charles Darwin. To all these men, the pinnacle of fame was to read a decisive paper before a scientific society. All were drawn to the giant river system of the Amazon by the incredible variety and quantity of plants, insects, reptiles and animals to be found there. They were looking for answers to a number of questions that had puzzled man for generations: does the earth bulge at the Equator? Why do some species perish? Why do others, in the face of identical natural onslaughts, survive? And they accepted extraordinary hardship, disease and danger to get the answers.

Explorer-scientists began arriving in the Amazon in the mid-18th Century, and increased in numbers in the 19th. They were by no means the first to penetrate these regions, which is perhaps one reason why they never achieved such great fame as the explorer-heroes of Africa. Quite a few of the basic facts about the Amazon had already been discovered by explorers in a more conventional mould over the preceding 250 years. The world's greatest river was discovered in 1500 by a Spanish skipper, Vicente Yañez Pinzón, who had voyaged with Columbus and, like Columbus, was seeking a route to the Indies. In 1541-42, another Spaniard, Captain Francisco de Orellana, became the first European to travel the entire length of the river. Starting in the river Coca in the foothills of the Ecuadorean Andes—which he had reached overland from the Pacific—he travelled tortuously downstream by way of the river Napo into the Upper Amazon, and thence more than 1,875 miles eastward to the Atlantic. He was also the first to bring back reports of the terrifying warrior women—the South American version of the Greek Amazons—after whom the river was named.

The chief problem faced by Orellana's expedition was hunger. The 60 sailors and soldiers in his boat—including a friar, Gaspar de Carvajal, who kept a record of the voyage—were reduced to eating their belts and the soles of their shoes boiled with herbs. They found themselves competing with the native Indians for the scarce food resources of the Amazon. Sometimes there were Indians willing to give them food. But at other times they raided villages to seize provisions, and it was during one such raid, probably near the mouth of the river Trombetas, between the middle and the lower Amazon, that they were attacked by a band of Indians. Among the warriors, Carvajal recorded, were a number of women, "very white and tall and having hair long and braided and wound about the head, and they are very robust and go about naked, but with their private parts covered." The report Orellana eventually took back to the King of Spain stated that these Amazons had "bows and arrows in their hands, with which they killed seven or eight Spaniards".

The most important large-scale expedition after Orellana's was undertaken by Pedro Teixeira, a Portuguese military commander, who travelled with a huge force of 2,000 men and 47 boats in 1637-38. Teixeira journeyed from Pará (now Belém) in Brazil, near the mouth of the Amazon, to Quito. He was the first to negotiate the length of the river upstream, slightly more than a century after Orellana had made the trip in the opposite direction. Then he went back down again. He was accompanied on his downstream trip by a Jesuit, Father Cristobal de Acuña, who left a vivid, analytical account of the journey and so established himself as a forerunner of the explorer-scientists.

During the century following Teixeira's expedition, when Europeans began to colonize the Amazon, great numbers of Indians died, possibly the majority then living within the basin. Some estimates say that as many as two million perished—in combat, as the result of enslavement or massacre and from disease. Malaria and yellow fever, probably brought by Europeans and by enslaved Africans imported by the Portuguese were bad enough, but the Indians were particularly susceptible to colds, as they still are. By the middle of the 18th Century, the Amazon basin was fairly peaceful—rather like a graveyard.

It was then that the first world-recognized scientist arrived. Charles Marie de la Condamine was a brilliant son of the Age of Reason, a friend of Voltaire and, at the age of 29, a member of the French Académie des Sciences. He was primarily a mathematician and a geodesist, but also a map-maker, a naturalist and an astronomer. His reason for visiting the Amazon was to help resolve a scientific dispute. Isaac Newton had promulgated the theory that the earth bulged at the Equator and flattened at the poles. French scientists argued exactly the opposite—that the poles bulged and the Equator flattened. The Académie despatched two teams to settle the matter, one to Lapland, and the second to Quito in South America. This latter one included La Condamine, as well as a botanist, an astronomer, a couple of mathematicians, a naval captain, a watch-maker and a doctor. La Condamine spent seven years helping prove, to the Académie's dismay (as the polar party also did), that Newton was right.

Then in 1743, he embarked on a two months' voyage from the Andes-fed river Marañón down the Amazon to the Atlantic. La Condamine studied the Amazon as no one had done before; and, thanks to his international prestige, what he said commanded immediate attention. His careful descriptions of the river—its depth, its fall, its rate of flow— and his report that the Amazon was probably connected by a natural canal to the Orinoco, opened a new era of exploration. His map of the

Alfred Wallace, a surveyor's assistant from the industrial Midlands of Victorian Britain, made himself a naturalist of world stature by his discoveries in the Amazon basin and later in the Far East. He worked out the theory of the origin of species at the same time as Charles Darwin.

river's trunk is still nearly as valid as when he drew it. La Condamine noted the natural fish-poisons and insecticides used by the Indians; investigated the properties of poison-arrows; described curare and collected quinine seeds and many other botanical specimens. Amazed by the bounce and elasticity of the coagulated fluid that oozed from the rubber tree, he took samples back to Paris, thus opening the way to a great new industry.

He also helped perpetuate the legend of the Amazons on the basis of tangible, if circumstantial, evidence. There is no record that he ever claimed to have found concrete proof of their existence. But he did see some of the green stones which Indians told him were the rewards the women gave to men who provided them with female children.

The Amazon explorers who followed La Condamine shared his passion for knowledge for its own sake. Probably the most famous of these explorer-scientists was the German naturalist, Friedrich Heinrich Alexander, Baron von Humboldt. It is recalled that Frederick the Great met Humboldt when he was 10 years old, and asked the boy if he meant to emulate his namesake, Alexander, and be a world-conqueror. "Yes, Sire," Humboldt replied, "but with my head."

In 1800, Humboldt travelled southward through Venezuela with his good friend, Aimé Bonpland, a French physician turned botanist. Their chief success was to confirm the existence of the so-called canal—actually a swift natural stream—said by La Condamine to link the Orinoco and the Amazon watersheds. Humboldt and Bonpland, after a voyage down the rushing Orinoco, their fragile little boat bobbing and bouncing in waters teeming with crocodiles, alligators and piranha, finally pinpointed the link. They also investigated rubber and curare, studied the piranha's habits and tested the voltage of the electric eel.

Scholarly explorers of many nationalities followed Humboldt. Although science ignores frontiers, there is an important reason for singling out the British at this point. By the mid-19th Century, Britain, largely as the result of the Industrial Revolution, was developing a new type of scientist. Learned men were no longer only wealthy aristocrats who could afford to dabble, but now came from lower middle-class families as well. They had to work for their own education, and had no means to travel unless they were paid to do so. Almost the only way botanists, entomologists and zoologists could earn money in the field was by collecting specimens—plants, insects, reptiles and warm-blooded animals. They could hope to be paid only a few pennies apiece for their finds, but if there were a great many new species in the region they chose, they could get by. The collections sent back to Britain were by far the biggest, because the British naturalists were the poorest and hungriest of the lot.

Alfred Russel Wallace, a former surveyor's assistant, and Henry Walter Bates, a hosier's apprentice, were perfect examples of the new breed of working-class, poverty-stricken explorers. Neither Wallace nor Bates had any formal scientific training and the account of what they achieved reads like one of the success stories so popular in the fiction of their own time. They met by chance in the provincial English town of Leicester, and in 1848, having saved about £100 each, they went to the Amazon. In May that year, these two young men, both in their early 20s, landed at Pará, now Belém. They would have looked like country cousins in any big city. Henry Bates was slight, shy, flitting and rather bird-like; Alfred Wallace was just short of six feet, gangling and myopic. No professional explorer on earth would have given them a hundred-to-one chance of surviving for more than a year, even here only on the periphery of the Green Hell, let alone within its depths.

HENRY BATES

In this frontier atmosphere, Bates and Wallace set themselves to fulfil commissions to supply rare plants and insects to the British Museum and to the botanist, Sir William Hooker, who built up both the Glasgow and the Kew botanical gardens. Every mounted insect, received in London in saleable condition, netted them just threepence. They rented a small house in the suburb of San Nazaré just outside Pará, and began to collect there, more or less in their own front garden, in order to make enough to pay their way further inland. At the end of only two months, they sent back to England examples of 1,300 different species of insects. Even more heartening was their realization that they had barely begun to tap the region's treasure-house of creatures unknown to science.

They then began to move out, first on to the river Tocantins, later further up the main Amazon channel, finally in Wallace's case, up the river Negro. Although they remained friends all their lives, they moved separately after the first four months. Neither mentions the reason why, but Bates may have gone a bit native. He had taken to dressing oddly—that is to say, comfortably—and he appears to have enjoyed the company of Indians and part-Indians more than that of his own people. Men of the British business community in Pará stopped raising their hats to him on the muddy streets, and he was regarded as rather eccentric as, no doubt, he was.

Wallace stayed in the Amazon for four years. But this period was possibly as productive in terms of man's knowledge of nature as any four years in the history of science. In the course of exploring the river Negro almost to its source, Wallace began to clarify and to develop the theory of evolution that he and Bates had jointly cherished almost from the start: that the characteristics of species evolve gradually over a period of time—rather than being created in their present form as related in Genesis.

It was only several years later that the explanation of what he had observed in South America came to him. He was by then on the tropical island of Ternate, in the Molucca Sea of Indonesia. Recovering from a fever, he was pondering why creatures should evolve when "it suddenly flashed upon me that this self-acting process would necessarily *improve the race*, because in every generation the inferior would inevitably be killed off and the superior would remain—that is, *the fittest would survive."*

He hurriedly wrote a paper and sent it off to a fellow naturalist who, Wallace knew, was working on the same problem—Charles Darwin. The two men's conclusions were strikingly alike, and Darwin faced a scholastic dilemma. He had almost completed but not yet published his famous book, *On the Origin of Species*, outlining his own theory of natural selection. Should he pretend he had never received Wallace's paper? Or should he share the inevitable acclaim? He finally decided on sharing, and on July 1, 1858, papers from both naturalists were read before a meeting of the Linnaean Society in London.

There was no question of jealousy on Wallace's part for the honours that later came to Darwin for his masterful exposition of evolution. As Wallace wrote to Bates, "... I could *never have approached* the completeness of his work, its vast accumulation of evidence, its overwhelming argument, and its admirable tone and spirit. I really feel thankful that it had *not* been left to me to give the theory to the world."

But it was left to Bates, as fine an entomologist as has ever lived, to show from his studies in the Amazon how natural selection actually works. He, too, made his research available to Darwin. Trying to discover why some creatures endure and others do not, he isolated two kinds of butterflies that resembled each other. One was palatable to birds, the other unpalatable. Why? His answer was what he called "mimetics". In order to survive, an animal must have a means of defence against predators, and some creatures found a defence in trickery. Thus successive generations of the palatable butterfly gradually assumed—imitated—the appearance of the butterfly that birds disliked. And birds, unable to tell the difference, left both alone, to live and reproduce. This mimetic principle, as Bates showed, was applied by all manner of living things: lizards that find protection in their resemblance to leaves or tree bark; pouncing spiders that curl up to look like flower buds.

It was a huge step forward in evolutionary theory. Bates guessed that the study of mimicry would one day be valued as one of the most important branches of biological science. Of the colour patterns on butterfly wings he noted: "On these expanded membranes Nature writes, as on a tablet, the story of the modifications of species."

Bates spent 11 years in the Amazon, during which he collected 14,712 species of mammals, birds, reptiles and insects, of which 8,000 were new to science. He was the world authority on ground beetles—which, in the Amazon, were tree beetles. Yet, towering as he was in his field, he may, in the end, be best remembered for his remarkable book, *The Naturalist on the River Amazons*. Its descriptions of animal and insect life are models of scientific precision, yet at the same time, delightful and strangely moving.

The sprightly little ex-hosier's apprentice travelled tirelessly up and down the river and through the surrounding forests, fortified by an almost childish love of nature and a belief that nothing would happen to him. Nothing did. His adventures were seldom heroic, but they were charged with his own strong sense of humanity which he extended, somehow, to all creature-life. In the deep forests around the Upper Amazon village of Ega, his favourite collecting-ground, he is attacked by a flock of curl-crested toucans; he crawls through the jungle litter looking for blind ants who travel beneath the leaves and never see the light, building covered earthen ways in order to cross a cleared space; anacondas wake him in the middle of the night, arousing no emotion but curiosity; he is sympathetic to bats; he tracks down enormous spiders and poisonous wasps; he takes respectful baths with alligators. Somehow, Bates makes one feel that these activities were not only normal, but almost humdrum. He was frequently shoeless and in rags, and, during one period, absolutely penniless. Yet he maintained a cheerful note.

While Wallace and Bates, both originally little more than amateur naturalists, were combing the Amazon for animal specimens which helped establish one of science's most significant advances, another Englishman, Richard Spruce, was investigating the characteristics of the tropical forest plants and building his reputation as one of the

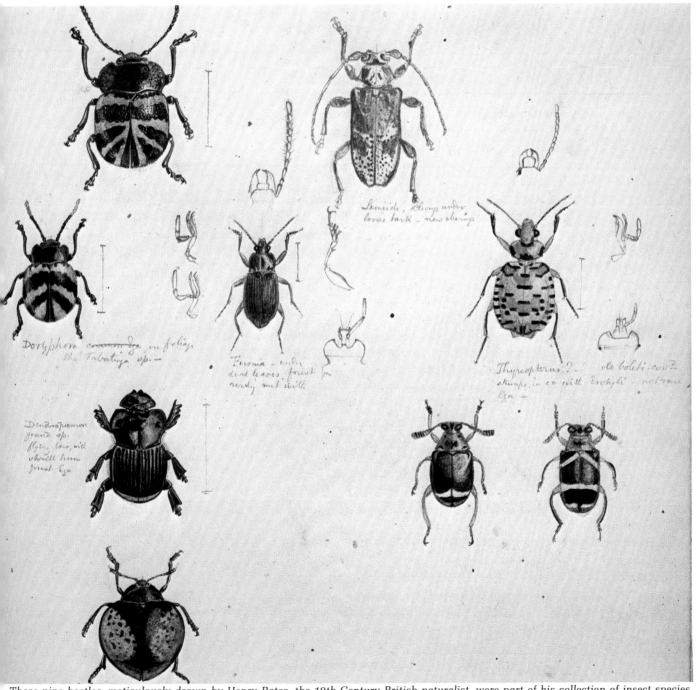

These nine beetles, meticulously drawn by Henry Bates, the 19th-Century British naturalist, were part of his collection of insect species.

world's finest botanists. Spruce, a Yorkshireman of 32, was also chiefly self-taught, but he had a slight advantage over Wallace and Bates in that he had gleaned some education from his father, who was a highly respected schoolmaster.

Spruce underwent physical trials which could have filled a heroic book of adventures. Once on the upper river Negro, racked with fever and diarrhoea, he staved off a night attack by four murderous, drunken Indians, staring them down with a double-barrelled shotgun, and a cutlass. When they sobered up, next morning, he even talked them into rowing him and his precious collection of plant specimens on towards his destination farther upriver.

RICHARD SPRUCE

Another time, on the Negro, near the Orinoco-Amazon canal which Humboldt had located, Spruce succumbed to fever. He had lodgings with a diabolical old woman who used to whisper at night, in the next room, "Die, you English dog, that we may have a merry watch-night with your money." But she may have saved his life. For all his graces, Spruce remained a tough Yorkshireman, and he determined to stay alive to spite the crone.

Throughout his illness, his scientific mind was working. He became his own doctor, refusing purges which were generally prescribed at that time for fever but probably killed as many people as did the malaria parasite. Spruce took quinine and ate what he could to gather strength. Slowly the fever passed, and the botanist went back to work.

Millions of people have had malaria, of course, and many have weathered it with great fortitude. But few, within days of the most severe period of their attacks, could have accomplished what Spruce did. He not only collected and mounted 29 plant species, but also wrote a short description of the collection area. At the peak of his fever, when he was nearly resigned to death, his one concern was how properly to dispose of his plant specimens. It was this degree of involvement in his work that enabled him to amass a collection of 7,000 important specimens during 17 years in the Amazon.

He spent the last 27 years of his life in two neat rooms in England, each about three yards square, on a pension that never exceeded £100 a year. He was so debilitated by his Amazon illness that he could not sit up in a chair for more than a few minutes at a time. He could hardly walk abroad for half an hour. He nevertheless obstinately lived to 76 and published a massive volume of 600 closely-printed pages on mosses: *Hepiticae of the Amazon and the Andes of Peru and Ecuador*. It is both an important work of scholarship and a record of great courage. Few people have risked their lives so resolutely for science.

Many other scientist-explorers, both amateur and professional, followed in the footsteps of Wallace, Bates and Spruce. Among the most important towards the end of the 19th Century were two married teams, Henri Anatole Coudreau, and his wife Olga; and Louis Agassiz, the great Swiss-American naturalist, and his wife, Elizabeth. The Coudreaus painstakingly mapped some of the river's larger tributaries and recorded their systematic and precise observations in books which have the arcadian charm of Bates's *The Naturalist on the River Amazons*. Louis and Elizabeth Agassiz also penetrated the wild regions, and described accurately what they had seen. Agassiz, who collected 2,000 species of fresh-water fish, reported that, in one pond smaller than a tennis court, he found more varieties than are contained in all the rivers of Europe combined—from the Tagus to the Volga.

There was one notable exception in the list of scientists, the Englishman Lieutenant Colonel P. H. Fawcett, D.S.O. He was the very archetype of the old-fashioned explorer-hero. In 1925, accompanied by his son and another youth, he deliberately abandoned the safety of the rivers and set out to walk through the wild jungles of the Mato Grosso, the region far south of the river Amazon in which no white man had set foot before. There Fawcett and the two young men simply disappeared. The case of the lost explorer was widely discussed in the newspapers. There were rumours the boys had died and that the Colonel, "maddened by grief", was wandering through the twilit forests, or had been struck down by "murderous Indians". Possibly they all died of simple starvation. But no one knew what happened, and probably no one ever will.

The explorers who followed in the 20th Century have continued the tradition of scientific discovery. Although today travel is somewhat less dangerous, there is still plenty of adventure in seeking previously un-recognized plants and animals. Despite the masses of data compiled by the pioneers of the past, the Amazon is still a wilderness. Much of its huge area is only vaguely known and thousands of species are still waiting for explorer-scientists to discover them.

Henry Bates, Searcher for Knowledge

The exotic world of the Amazon acted as a magnet to European explorers, buccaneers and traders from the 16th Century onwards. In the 18th Century, it attracted increasing numbers of scientists and, by the mid-19th Century, it had become a hunting ground for naturalists who began cataloguing the thousands of species of flora and fauna to be found there.

The best of these naturalists were British, young, self-taught and intensely curious. The one who had best claim to know the world of the Amazon was Henry Walter Bates who spent 11 years of his life there, from 1848 to 1859. He made his name by publishing a book of his travels, *The Naturalist on the River Amazons*. His delightfully vivid style captured the Victorian imagination and earned the praise of numerous writers including Charles Darwin, Charles Kingsley and, later, D. H. Lawrence and George Orwell. Extracts from his writing, illustrated by his own intricate drawings, are reproduced on the following pages.

Bates was the son of a hosier in the industrial Midlands of England and he had no capital to finance his explorations. Instead, he supported himself by selling specimens, mostly of insects, to British museums and private collectors for threepence each.

In all, he collected more than 14,000 species, of which 8,000 were new to science. From these Charles Darwin drew evidence to support his revolutionary theory of natural selection as the basis of evolution.

Bates collected specimens from nine each morning until two in the afternoon, enjoying himself "amazingly", as he wrote in a letter to his brother. "Over my left shoulder slings my double-barrelled gun. In my right hand I take my net; on my left side is suspended a leather bag with two pockets, one for my insect box, the other for powder and two sorts of shot; on my right hand hangs my "game bag", an ornamental affair, with red leather trappings and thongs to hang lizards, snakes, frogs, or large birds; one small pocket in this bag contains my caps, another papers for wrapping up delicate birds . . . to my shirt is pinned my pin cushion, with six sizes of pins."

In the frontispiece to his book, the naturalist, Henry Bates, depicts "an amusing adventure" when he was besieged by toucans near the river Solimoes. He had attempted to shoot the only toucan visible when, "as if by magic, the shady nook seemed alive with these birds . . . all croaking and fluttering their wings like so many furies."

A Naturalist's Notebook

FLAT-TOPPED MOUNTAINS

"About midnight the wind, for which we had long been waiting, sprang up, the men weighed anchor, and we were soon fairly embarked on the Amazons. I rose long before sunrise to see the great river by moonlight. There was a spanking breeze, and the vessel was bounding gaily over the waters. The channel along which we were sailing was only a narrow arm of the river, about two miles in width: the total breadth at this point is more than 20 miles, but the stream is divided into three parts by a series of large islands. The river, notwithstanding this limitation of its breadth, had a most majestic appearance. It did not present that lake-like aspect which the waters of the Pará and Tocantins [rivers] affect, but had all the swing, so to speak, of a vast flowing stream . . . with an horizon of water and sky both upstream and down. . . . A chain of blue hills, the Serra de Almeyrim, appeared in the distance on the north bank of the river. The sight was most exhilarating after so long a sojourn in a flat country. . . . The hills . . . are about 800 feet above the level of the river and are thickly wooded to the summit. They commence on the east by a few low isolated and rounded elevations; but towards the west of the village [Almeyrim] they assume the appearance of elongated ridges, which seem to have been planed down to a uniform height by some external force. . . .

"We used to make our halt in a small cleared place, tolerably free from ants and close to the water.

Here we assembled after the toilsome morning's hunt in different directions through the woods, took our well-earned meal on the ground—two broad leaves of the wild banana serving us for a table cloth—and rested for a couple of hours during the great heat of the afternoon. . . . A number of large, fat lizards two feet long, of a kind called by the natives Jacuarú (Teius teguexim) were always observed in the still hours of midday scampering with great clatter over the dead leaves, apparently in chase of each other. . . . The lazy flapping flight of large blue and black morpho butterflies high in the air, the hum of insects, and many inanimate sounds, contributed their share to the total impression this strange solitude produced. Heavy fruits from the crowns of trees which were mingled together at a giddy height overhead, fell now and then with a startling 'plop' into the water. The breeze, not felt below, stirred in the topmost branches, setting the twisted and looped sipós [vines] in motion, which creaked and groaned in a great variety of notes. . . . [We] came upon a treeless space choked up with tall grass, which appeared to be the dried-up bed of another lake. Our leader was obliged to climb a tree to ascertain our position, and found that the clear space was part of the creek, whose mouth we had crossed lower down. The banks were clothed with low trees, nearly all of one species, a kind of araça (Psidium) [Brazilian guava], and the ground was carpeted with a slender delicate grass, now in flower. A great number of crimson and vermilion-coloured butterflies (Catagramma Peristera, male and female) were settled on the smooth, white trunks of these trees. I had also here the great pleasure of seeing for the first time the rare and curious Umbrella Bird (Cephalopterus ornatus), a species which

UMBRELLA BIRD

resembles in size, colour and appearance our common crow, but is decorated with a crest of long, curved, hairy feathers having long bare quills, which, when raised, spread themselves out in the form of a fringed sunshade over the head. A strange ornament, like a pelerine, is also suspended from the neck, formed by a thick pad of glossy steel-blue feathers, which grow on a long fleshy lobe or excrescence. . . . We had the good luck, after remaining quiet a short time, to hear its performance. It drew itself up on its perch, spread widely the umbrella-formed crest, dilated and waved its glossy breast-lappet, and then, in giving vent to its loud piping note, bowed its head slowly forwards. . . .

"In the course of our walk I chanced to verify a fact relating to the habits of a large hairy spider of the genus Mygale, in a manner

JACUARU LIZARD

worth recording. . . .The individual was nearly two inches in length of body, but the legs expanded seven inches, and the entire body and legs were covered with coarse grey and reddish hairs. I was attracted by a movement of the monster on a tree-trunk; it was close beneath a deep crevice in the tree, across which was stretched a dense white web. The lower part of the web was broken, and two small birds, finches, were entangled in the pieces; they were about the size of the English siskin, and I judged the two to be male and female. One of them was quite dead, the other lay under the body of the spider not quite dead, and was smeared with the filthy liquor or saliva exuded by the monster. I drove away the spider and took the birds, but the second one soon died. . . . Some Mygales are of immense size. One day I saw the children belonging to an Indian family who collected for me with one of these monsters secured by a cord round its waist, by which they were leading it about the house as they would a dog. . . .

"One night my servant woke me at three or four hours before sunrise by calling out that the rats were rob-

SAUBA ANT

HAIRY SPIDER

bing the farinha [tapioca] baskets; the article at that time being scarce and dear. I got up, listened, and found the noise was very unlike that made by rats. So I took the light and went into the storeroom, which was close to my sleeping place. I there found a broad column of Sauba ants, consisting of thousands of individuals, as busy as possible, passing to and fro between the door and my precious baskets. Most of those passing outwards were laden each with a grain of farinha, which was, in some cases, larger and many times heavier than the bodies of the carriers. Farinha consists of grains of similar size and appearance to the tapioca of our shops; both are products of the same root, tapioca being the pure starch, and farinha the starch mixed with woody fibre,

the latter ingredient giving it a yellowish colour. It was amusing to see some of the dwarfs, the smallest members of their family, staggering along, completely hidden under their load. The baskets, which were on a high table, were entirely covered with ants, many hundreds of whom were employed in snipping the dry leaves which served as lining. This produced the rustling sound which had at first disturbed us. My servant told me that they would carry off the whole contents of the two baskets (about two bushels) in the course of the night, if they were not driven off; so we tried to exterminate them by killing them with our wooden clogs. It was impossible, however, to prevent fresh hosts coming in as fast as we killed their companions. They returned the next night; and I was then obliged to lay trains of gunpowder along their line, and blow them up. This, repeated many times, at last seemed to intimidate them....

"A strange kind of wood-cricket is found in this neighbourhood [near Obydos]. The males produce a very loud and not unmusical noise by rubbing together the overlapping edges of their wing-cases. The notes are certainly the loudest and most extraordinary that I ever heard produced by an orthopterous insect. The natives call it the Tananá, in allusion to its music, which is a sharp, resonant stridulation resembling the syllables ta-na-ná, ta-

na-ná, succeeding each other with little intermission. It seems to be rare in the neighbourhood. When the natives capture one they keep it in a wicker-work cage for the sake of hearing it sing. A friend of mine kept one six days. It was lively only for two or three, and then its loud note could be heard from one end of the village to the other....

"The number of spiders ornamented with showy colours was somewhat remarkable. Some double themselves up at the base of leaf-stalks, so as to resemble flowerbuds, and thus deceive the insects on which they prey. The most extra-

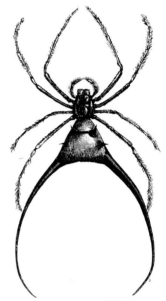

ACROSOMA SPIDER

ordinary-looking spider was a species of Acrosoma, which had two curved bronze-coloured spines, an inch and a half in length, proceeding from the tip of its abdomen. It spins a large web, the monstrous appendages being apparently no impediment to it in its work; but what their use can be I am unable to divine....

"The population of the water varied from day to day. Once a small shoal of a handsome black-banded fish, called by the natives, Acará bandeira, ... came gliding through at a slow pace, forming a very pretty sight. At another time, little troops of needle fish, eel-like animals, with excessively long and slender toothed jaws, sailed through the field, scattering before them the hosts of smaller fry; and in the rear of

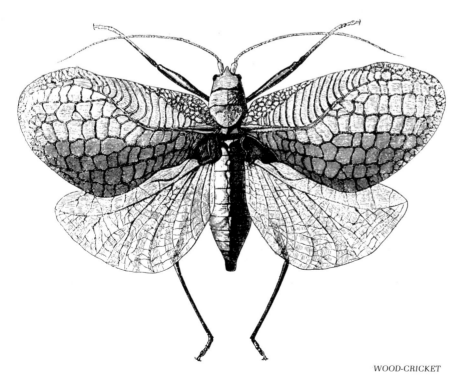

WOOD-CRICKET

BATES PREPARING TO KILL AN ALLIGATOR

the needle-fishes a strangely-shaped kind called Sarapó came wriggling along, one by one, with a slow movement. We caught with hook and line, baited with pieces of banana, several Curimatá (Anodus Amazonum) a most delicious fish, which, next to the Tucunaré and the Pescada, is most esteemed by the natives. . . .

"On the 6th of October we left Ega [on the river Solimoes] on a second excursion; the principle object . . . being this time, to search certain pools in the forest for young turtles. . . . When the net was formed into a circle and the men had jumped [into the water to direct the turtles], an alligator was found to be enclosed. No one was alarmed, the only fear expressed being that the imprisoned beast would tear the net. First one shouted, "I have touched his head;" then another, "he has scratched my leg." One of the men, a lanky Miranha, was thrown off his balance, and then there was no end to the laughing and shouting. At last a youth of about fourteen years of age, on my calling to him from the bank, to do so, seized the reptile by the tail, and held him tightly until, a little resistance being overcome, he was able to bring it ashore. The net was opened, and the boy slowly dragged the dangerous but cowardly

NEEDLE FISH

beast to land through the muddy water, a distance of about one hundred yards. Meantime, I had cut a strong pole from a tree, and as soon as the alligator was drawn to solid ground, gave him a smart rap with it on the crown of his head, which killed him instantly. It was a good-sized individual; the jaws being considerably more than a foot long, and fully capable of snapping a man's leg in twain. The species was the large cayman, the Jacaré-uassú of the Amazonian Indians. . . .

"The natives at once despise and fear the great cayman. I once spent a month at Caiçara, a small village of semi-civilized Indians, about twenty miles to the west of Ega. . . .

"A large trading canoe . . . arrived at this time, and the Indian crew, as usual, spent the first day or two after their coming in port, in drunkenness and debauchery ashore. One of the men, during the greatest heat of the day when almost everyone was enjoying his afternoon's nap, took it into his head whilst in a tipsy state to go down alone to bathe. He was seen only by the Juiz de Paz, a feeble old man who was lying in his hammock, in the open verandah at the rear of his house on the top of the bank, and who shouted to the besotted Indian to beware of the alligator. Before he could repeat his warning, the man stumbled, and a pair of gaping jaws, appearing suddenly from the surface, seized him round the waist and drew him under the water. A

cry of 'Ai Jesús!' was the last sign made by the wretched victim. . . .

"On emerging from the Uituquára [near the mouth of the Amazon] we all went ashore—the men to fish in a small creek; Joaõ da Cunha and I to shoot birds. We saw a flock of scarlet and blue macaws (Macrocercus macao) feeding on the

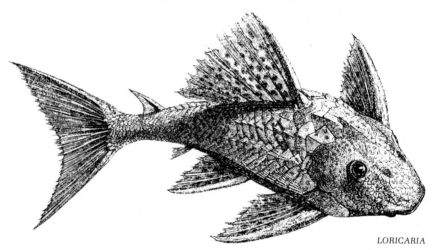

LORICARIA

fruits of a Bacaba palm, and looking like a cluster of flaunting banners beneath its dark-green crown. We landed about fifty yards from the place and crept cautiously through the forest, but before we reached them they flew off with loud harsh screams. At a wild-fruit tree we were more successful, as my companion shot an anacá (Derotypus coronatus), one of the most beautiful of the parrot family. . . . The men returned with a large quantity of fish. I was surprised at the great variety of species; the prevailing kind was a species of Loricaria, a

foot in length and wholly encased in bony armour. . . .

"On each side [of the creek] were the tops of bushes and young trees, forming a kind of border to the path, and the trunks of the tall forest trees rose at irregular intervals from the water, their crowns interlocking far over our heads and

forming a thick shade. Slender air roots hung down in clusters and looping sipós dangled from the lower branches; bunches of grasses, tillandsiae, and ferns sat in the forks of the larger boughs, and the trunks of the trees near the water had adhering to them round dried masses of fresh-water sponges. There was no current perceptible, and the water was stained of a dark olive-brown hue, but the submerged stems could be seen through it to a great depth. We travelled at good speed for three hours along this shady road. . . . When the paddlers rested for a time, the stillness and gloom of the place became almost painful; our voices waked dull echoes as we conversed, and the noise made by fishes occasionally whipping the surface of the water was quite startling. . . . We often read in books of travels of the silence and gloom of the Brazilian forests. They are realities, and the impression deepens on a longer acquaintance. The few sounds of the birds are of that pensive or mysterious character which intensifies the feeling of solitude rather than imparts a sense of life and cheerfulness.

"Sometimes in the midst of the stillness, a sudden yell or scream will startle one; this comes from some defenceless fruit-eating animal, which is pounced upon by a tiger cat or stealthy boa constrictor. Morning and evening the howling monkeys make a most fearful and harrowing noise under which it is difficult to keep up one's buoyancy of spirit. . . .

"There are, besides, many sounds which it is impossible to account for. . . . Sometimes a sound is heard like the clang of an iron bar against a hard, hollow tree, or a piercing cry rends the air; these are not repeated, and the succeeding silence tends to heighten the unpleasant impression which they make on the mind. With the natives it is always the Curupíra, the wild man or spirit of the forest, which produces all noises they are unable to explain."

PRIMEVAL FOREST

6/ People of the Jungle

---

*The Indian of Amazonia . . . lives in unmediated
contact with nature, and this is what makes him one of
the most primitive of all men.* EMIL SCHULTHESS/THE AMAZON

The chief danger man faces in the Amazon is not the piranha, anaconda
or any other over-dramatized monster of the Green Hell, but hunger and
disease. The law of the rain forest decrees that the larger an animal
is, the harder its survival becomes; and by Amazon standards, man is
a very large animal indeed. Most Europeans cut off from outside
supplies—as Colonel Fawcett no doubt discovered on his final journey
into the jungle—are quickly threatened by starvation. But native
Indian tribes have no outside supplies, and yet survive and frequently
eat quite well. How? The answer is a fascinating, and in some ways
horrifying revelation of how man must behave if he is to live in harmony
with nature in a tropical rain forest.

As a direct result of the lack of food, Amazon Indian groups are
rare and small and many are thoroughly homicidal. They are widely
scattered—like all higher animals in the forest—and with few
exceptions they live in communities of not more than two or three
hundred. Beyond that number—or even well before—the lack of
food in the immediate neighbourhood forces the group to split. As
the groups—really just extended families—thrust outwards in their
desperate search for food, they come into conflict with each other.
It is simply not true, as romantically inclined outsiders have claimed,
that all Indians feel themselves to be brothers-of-the-forest, whose
only enemy is the white man. An Indian's greatest human enemy is

another Indian. In isolated tribes—for example, the Yanoáma in the north, near the Amazon-Orinoco divide, and the Jivarós in the foothills of the Andes—close on half the male population end their lives violently, most of them in tribal warfare. As a result, the population tends to become predominantly female in composition. The Jivarós, who are head hunters and head shrinkers, have only about one man to every two women.

If this seems brutal and senseless, the answer is, yes, it is brutal, but it makes sense. A number of observers think the Amazon Indians' whole system of war and violence has the effect of keeping the population level down, matching the number of eaters to the forest's food resources. The internecine Jivarós maintain a stable population of about one person to every one and a quarter square miles, and this is apparently the number their area can sustain.

There never were very many Indians in the Amazon forests—probably no more than three million at any time during the past 15,000 years, the period during which they are known to have lived here. But now there are not more than 100,000 at the outside, and possibly as few as 50,000. The decline has been caused, not by the forest, but by a threat to which they cannot adapt: the white man. The first Europeans the Indians encountered were 16th-Century Spanish and Portuguese conquistadors; they brought firearms, diseases and Christian doctrines, more or less in that order. Each had a profound effect on the indigenous population. The firearms, used by the Europeans to defend themselves— and to discourage the Indians from defending *themselves*—killed selectively. Smallpox, syphilis, measles and the common cold were eventually far more lethal, destroying whole families and decimating tribes. Christianity had a more subtle effect: it often destroyed the native culture. So that, even when the Indians survived physically, they often met a death of the spirit.

The long and continuing European encroachment has been far more disastrous to the Indians than any amount of internecine tribal warfare and feuding. The few surviving tribes have either retreated beyond the rapids of the Amazon tributaries, taking shelter in the last few untouched wilderness areas of the Guyana and Brazilian rock shields, or they have been herded into tribal reserves. Since most of the Amazon forests are in Brazil, it is Brazil's National Indian Foundation (FUNAI) that holds responsibility for most of the remaining tribes and from which I obtained permission to visit the Yanoáma Indians far north of the river Amazon and study their stone-age culture.

This was the final purpose of my trip up the river Catrimani, after gaining some experience of Amazonian geology in the rapids and the personal botany lesson of a walk in the forest. The upper reaches of the Catrimani, like those of other northern tributaries of the river Negro, stretch far up in the ancient rock shield on the borders of Brazil and Venezuela. All along the edges of the Amazon basin, and especially here in the north, civilization has been kept at bay by rapids and falls. Consequently, the area beyond the rapids is one of the wildest places on earth. In 12,000 square miles—equivalent to a third of Ireland—there is nothing but the endless forest, the thousand Yanoáma aborigines who now roam it and a tiny Roman Catholic mission station. The mission, at Cujubim Falls near the Serra da Pimenta, was to be the base for my stay among the Yanoáma. To reach it, I had to go through the obstacle course of nearly all the rapids on the river Catrimani. Luckily, the four men of Indian and mixed race who had brought me through the lower rapids were continuing upriver with supplies for the mission station, and I was glad to go with them.

Father Giovanni Saffirio, who ran the mission single handed and whose impetuous hospitality I enjoyed at Cujubim Falls, was an energetic man in his mid-thirties. He was one of those fresh, green shoots of a Church that has been renewing itself for 2,000 years in the most improbable situations. His preoccupation was with the welfare of the Indians and he was bent on helping them adapt to the pressures that threaten their culture. It was no simple task—the mission station had only been here five years, and the previous head of it, Father Callerie, had been killed.

Fortunately for both the Father and myself, there was—for the moment—an uncharacteristic degree of peace. The tribal group I visited, along with some neighbouring groups, were recent immigrants to this area. They had been driven out of their former country around the upper river Demini by another more powerful faction of the same tribe and were still on reasonably good terms with each other.

The first thing that surprised me about the Yanoáma was that, with death constantly impinging on their lives, they are not philosophically resigned to it. On the contrary, they do not accept that death can ever be natural or even accidental. If there is no obvious cause, such as a wound, they explain a death as a result of a spell. In a sense all their people die violently, if one will admit that evil spells are violent. Sickness and death through disease are thought to be the result of someone's bad wishes, and all such acts of aggression must be avenged if possible: the culprit identified, his malevolence punished.

One morning, as we were walking down towards the tribal lodge, or *maloca*, I asked Father Giovanni about the belief that death cannot be accidental, recalling that I had read the idea was practically universal here in the Amazon, among the forest peoples.

"Yes," he said, in staccato Piedmontese Italian, "it seems to be true. It's a bit like—well, at home, still, in some places in the country. . . ."

He didn't seem to want to finish the sentence. "You mean the Evil Eye?" I said.

"Yes, exactly."

I mentioned that I had come across something like this in the Abruzzo mountains, north-east of Rome; and that, from what I had been told, the Evil Eye was always attributed to envy.

He nodded. "I think so. I've heard that. And that seems to be true, here, as well. People are very afraid of envy. And . . . well, I think that makes them generous. They are a generous people, you know. If I give a man a machete in payment for some work he's likely to give it away within a week because somebody else has envied it. He just *gives* it away, because . . . well, I suppose he's afraid."

We passed a young man carrying a small bundle of wood, probably for a household fire. Father Giovanni leaped at him and put a hand to his forehead. They spoke for a minute in the boy's language, and then we went on. "He's better now. Sometimes they'll take my medicines, and sometimes they won't. He wouldn't. I don't force anyone, except for Raimundo, the one with tuberculosis. That isn't his real name, of course. They won't give me their real names. I mean that nobody uses a man's true name to his face—unless he's an enemy. An enemy shouts it. Knowing a man's name gives you power over him, you see. A friend, therefore, may know your name but it isn't polite to use it openly. So I call him Raimundo. We were saying? Yes. I don't force medicines on anyone, except for Raimundo. He was down river for a while, near a settlement. By the time he came back he was nearly dead. I *had* to force him then. We've got him in a separate hut, of course, and his food is prepared separately."

For the Father, action of this sort would come under the heading of Christian charity. But, clearly, there were dangers involved. Among people who think of sickness as being the result of someone's bad wishes, any attempt to cure them may also be confused with the cause of their illness. In dispensing medicines he always ran a certain risk and he was well aware that failure might mark him as a murderer.

He was happy to interfere with traditional practices for the sake of the Indians' health, but not otherwise. He would never for instance have tried to break the long established patterns of marriage, which are somewhat complicated. Most marriages among the Yanoáma are monogamous, but established heads of families and influential men often have a number of wives, sometimes as many as five. Though families are frequently polygamous, they can also be polyandrous. If a couple have a number of still-born children or children born deformed (the latter are usually killed at once) the wife will be encouraged to seek a child from some other man, preferably a young, unmarried one.

As a result, adultery has little meaning. "When a man comes to stay with a family," the Father told me, "he ties up his hammock with them and his host—ah, offers his wife. A form of hospitality. You have to see it in that light, I think. Of course, the woman doesn't always agree, and that can cause trouble. An uncharitable act."

Yanoáma marriage customs appear not so much to dictate what one should do as what one should not do. Quite simply, anything we would call incest—including marriage between parallel cousins—is forbidden. Marriages between cross-cousins—that is with the children of the brother of one's mother—are encouraged; and practically any other sort of arrangement is allowed. Homosexual relationships are rare, and are strongly disapproved of.

All this sounds a perfectly reasonable way to regulate the pairing-off of human beings, but there is another form of marriage that causes great dissension. Women are often abducted from other tribes. Some of them become the wives of their captors. They are the fortunate ones. Quite a few are kept aside as prostitutes and treated as something less than human, although they may later be taken in marriage.

One might think that abduction and war would go hand-in-hand. Not so: sometimes the abduction is almost a peaceful operation. The abducted woman will scream and call for help and her relatives will try to defend her, but not with arrows. She can also be snatched back again and then her original kidnappers will try to keep her, also using any weapon but arrows. The exchange may eventually be worked out through negotiations and the abducted bride may even be satisfied with the arrangement. Only if further violence stems from this rough wooing does war result.

We came in sight of the *maloca*. It was a huge structure, almost circular, about 100 yards in diameter and possibly 100 feet high. It

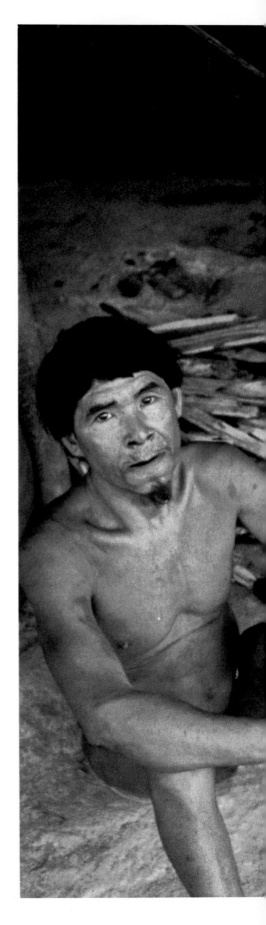

Lazing in their tribal lodge in northern Brazil, Yanoáma Indians look up at the camera with a mixture of nonchalance and apprehension.

was made of palm fibres and dry leaves, woven on a skeleton of poles, and shaped into a dome at the top. It gave an immediate impression of unity, of co-ordinated effort. It was a truly tremendous achievement for a small group of people with almost no tools to have managed by themselves. How, for instance, did they ever finish off the top without someone being killed?

As we walked down the path, which led directly to one of the doors, I was marvelling at the disciplined work which had gone into the structure, when Father Giovanni told me that it had been built with no discipline at all. The *maloca* had begun, he said, when one or two families built a protecting wall on one side, and others living near them continued the wall, which bent rather naturally into a circle. Then a few constructed higher walls, leaning inwards and held up by poles. Other groups followed, building higher still. No one family had any intention of doing work for anyone else—they took care of their own. Eventually a point was reached where very tall central poles had to be put up to keep the whole structure from collapsing. Two or three men would try to set up a centre pole, and others would sit around watching them, until they demonstrated how helpless they were. Seeing this the other men would break out laughing and finally get up to help. And, at last, it would be done.

"You see," said Father Giovanni, indicating the interior circular wall, "each family has its own position, where they hang their hammocks and keep their belongings. They live apart, but all together." It was like being in a giant beehive; the room was so dim that it was almost impossible to see across it. It was nearly deserted, since most of the men had gone out on a hunting expedition. But as my eyes grew used to the darkness I saw that some of the nearby hammocks were occupied. Some people were resting, but others appeared to be ill. The Father went to ask them how they were feeling. Most of them turned away or were not very responsive. The place reminded me of an army barracks. People who have togetherness and a collective life thrust upon them are not very enthusiastic about it except when they are having parties.

A party, if that is the right word, is one of the most important social activities of the Yanoáma. Father Giovanni told me that several times a year neighbouring tribes who are at peace with each other exchange festive visits. The invited tribe arrive in ceremonial dress. The women decorate their bodies with red *urucu* juice on which they make designs in black, and the men wear hats of white feathers and armbands of toucan feathers. They make a relatively friendly approach, carefully pointing their bows and arrows away from their hosts, but they can point them at their hosts very quickly if the need should arise. The two headmen sing ceremonial songs and the festivities begin.

Alcoholic beverages are not used by the Yanoáma. They prefer a kind of hallucinogenic snuff called *epená*, which is made from various plants. There seem to be at least two kinds: one is made from the bark of several related trees, mixed with aromatic leaves; and the other is made from the seeds of mimosa acaioides. It is also known as *parica*, *yupa* and *niopo* and used by many tribes of the Lower Amazon and the river Japura. Among the Yanoáma, *epená* is taken only by men.

The interesting thing about the drug itself and the festivals at which it is taken is that it appears to be an aid to working off aggressions. *Epená*, like other hallucinatory drugs, is often associated with peace. However, the Yanoáma act anything but peacefully when they take it (the powder is blown up their nostrils through a long tube). It produces a kind of drunkenness, without the staggers, and encourages visions. Under the influence of *epená*, the men hold various contests which stylize and channel violence and aggression. They may kneel before each other, for instance, and exchange blows across the chest with an open hand. Sometimes, especially if there has been a quarrel between the parties, they strike each other on the crown of the head with clubs— one for you, one for me, one for you, etc. The man who endures the longest wins.

This ritual is, of course, carrying peace right to the brink of war. But no man dare kill his opponent because he is surrounded by relatives, all of them armed. This requires rather fine judgement: if you do not hit hard enough you lose and if you hit too hard you lose.

Epená is not, therefore, something to be taken casually, as alcohol might be taken at a rowdy party. Moreover, apart from working off aggression, it has a further, religious significance. It is used in masculine initiation ceremonies, and is connected with ritual magic and the calling-up of spirits. It is also used by shamans for curing illnesses which, to the Indians, means casting out evil spirits.

To these ritualistic social occasions, heightened by the use of hallucinatory drugs, we must add another element in order to understand the Indian way of life: one that is apparent to anyone who has passed any time in the Amazon forests—loneliness. When a person can expect to see no more than a few hundred people as long as he lives, he is naturally overcome by the immensity of the world around him, and by his own relative insignificance within it. One can imagine therefore the effect a native festival has on an Indian child, living practically alone in the middle of this vast green universe.

At the close of these festivals—or some of them—people also eat their own dead. This may sound repulsive to us, but the ceremony is extremely touching, and not the least uncouth or unhygienic. When a man, woman or child dies, the body is either burned or exposed in a tree until only the dry bones are left. These are gathered and charred; the residue is reduced to a fine powder in a mortar (great care being taken not to leave any splinters of bone, which could stick in the throat) and, when needed, it is mixed with banana pap, and eaten. This is a duty which every living person owes to his forebears, in order to liberate the spirit. In fact, a living person can be threatened by his own relations who might say—under extreme provocation—that if he does not behave, they will not eat his bones. He will thus be condemned to a miserable and restless after-life, unable to return to the House of Thunder, to live in eternal youth. The Yanoáma regard burial in the ground as barbarous and, in the worst sense of the word, savage.

The Indians' way of life may not endure much longer. As European encroachment continues, they are driven from their tribal lands, displaced and harassed. Their numbers will no doubt dwindle further, through disease, genocide and their own internecine tribal wars. Their future looks dim: privately the Brazilian government admits that it would be most convenient were they to disappear and General Jeronomo O. Bandeirad de Melo, head of the FUNAI, has said openly that "assistance for the Indians cannot be allowed to obstruct national development".

Even those who try desperately to help may, paradoxically, contribute to the decline of the Indians. The Villas Boas brothers have worked devotedly for the Indians with other members of their family for 30 years, yet recently they announced they were retiring from the Amazon and, by implication, from their work with the National Indian Foundation. For, as they said, "we are convinced that every time we contact a tribe we are contributing towards the destruction of the purest things that tribe possesses."

Even Father Giovanni and his good intentions may contribute to the decline, even disappearance, of the Indian way of life. By his very presence among the Indians, however much he respects their traditions, he constitutes a force for change. He has to be, to cushion the

Indians against the inevitable, overwhelming impact of civilization.

In one respect—at least when I saw him—he was determined to enforce change. He had developed a system of cards to be given out for work and which were exchangeable for goods. The trouble was that he could not define "work"—no word for it existed in the Indians' language. He had finally settled for a word that more or less indicated "weeding". He wanted people to weed their gardens and was ready to pay them with little cards to weed his. There was not much point in this, perhaps, and no one would weed for more than an hour or two in the early morning, but he was trying to put across the idea of work. This, as he admitted, was not necessarily the ultimate virtue but it was, nevertheless, a law of the outside world that could destroy the Indians if they did not know about it.

Listening to the Father, I was not at all sure whether his system would protect the Indians or merely help them to accept the extinction of their way of life. If a road were pushed through this district— as some day it almost surely would be—the culture of these Yanoáma Indians would be slowly and inevitably destroyed. Even if a fence were to be built around them, no matter how well it was guarded (and it would not be well guarded), life on the inside would become a mere caricature of itself.

I did not know whether his work would make much difference or not. This was not Father Giovanni's fault nor, in the long view, was it anybody's fault. People who regret the cultural extinction of these stone-age Indians fail to suggest any way their cultures can be preserved. Ideally, from the Indians' point of view, the Amazon should never have been invaded at all. But it has been invaded and so it becomes the moral duty of every Amazonian government to give the Indians as much protection as possible while they are passing into a new culture. For this purpose men such as Father Giovanni are extremely valuable.

In the meantime, the Indians have a good deal to teach the rest of us. They have survived in this world against almost unimaginable odds. One day, if or when our own environment gets out of hand, we may well regret that we have not gone to them to be taught as well as to teach, to receive from their cultures as well as to impose our own.

Life in a Forest Village

PHOTOGRAPHS BY HARALD SCHULTZ

The Amazon forest is strangely empty of human life. The 100,000 Indians scattered over $2\frac{1}{2}$ million square miles are its only inhabitants outside the few oases of white civilization in the isolated river ports. The number of Indians today is a mere fraction of what it was at the beginning of the 16th Century when the first white explorers, eager to exploit the apparently limitless riches of the forest, introduced European diseases that decimated whole tribes. But the 150 linguistically isolated tribes that remain show how men can learn to live in harmony with nature, in the demanding, often hostile environment of the Amazonian rain forest.

Their life-style has hardly changed from the time they migrated from North America to become the area's first inhabitants about 15,000 years ago. Those who have escaped the disruptive effects of Western intrusion still live in villages of about 60 people. They are wholly dependent on the forest from which they cull their limited needs.

While they engage in some hunting and fishing, their chief occupation is cultivating mandioca, a native form of the cassava root, from which they make cakes, soup and even beer. They also grow maize, cotton and tobacco. They use the "slash-and-burn" method to form ragged clearings, felling the trees with stone axes and burning the undergrowth. After two years, when the soil fertility is exhausted, the old plot is abandoned and a new one cleared.

But the forest fulfils more than the basic need for food. It also provides a string of ancillary products used by the Indians to vary and enrich their lives. They extract salt from water hyacinths by burning the plant, leaching out the salt with water and boiling it down to a crystalline powder of potash and potassium chloride, a bitter-tasting cousin of common salt.

From the forest they have evolved an extensive pharmacopoeia including contraceptives, poisons and hallucinogenic drugs. A drink distilled, appropriately, from the passion flower, appears to stop ovulation the way modern oral contraceptives do. The *Strychnos* vine provides curare, the deadly poison used on arrow heads, while the *Banisteriopsis*, another vine, produces an hallucinogenic drug that, the Indians believe, induces visions returning them to "the source of all things".

Men of the Uruku Indians, living near the river Madeira, build a maloca, or communal house, by binding to a pole frame palm-fronds that have been stripped in half. The frond stems form a lattice, the leaves a thick spongy wall. A red dye called urucu may be smeared on the roof to ward off evil spirits.

The Village Commune

Scattered through the Amazon are hundreds of Indian villages, isolated by the forest and almost perfectly self-contained.

Life in most of them is almost exclusively communal. The 60 or so inhabitants share living space in the large palm-thatch *malocas* encircling the village "square", three or four families to each. Individuals may own the odd gourd or cooking bowl, some hunting gear and the arm and leg bands that serve as clothes. But in most villages, they share the land, their labour and the food they produce. The villagers assign the daily jobs among themselves with the chief, the village counsellor and co-ordinator, stepping in to smooth over any disruptive bickering.

As the men disperse deep into the forest to hunt and gather foods, some women wander off to cultivate crops in the ragged clearings surrounding the village, while others stay behind to prepare food, weave and care for the children.

Contact with neighbouring villages is limited to the occasional festival and the desultory bartering of excess goods.

An aerial view of a village of the Waura Indians in the Xingu region, south of the river Amazon, shows malocas *arranged around an open space. The open-sided building on the left is an exclusive male club. The white mounds are flour prepared from the mandioca root.*

Women of the Maku tribe, located near the river Negro, make a coarse, white flour by pounding, grating and sifting pupunha coconut. The same method is used to prepare the staple mandioca root, except that its poisonous prussic acid has to be squeezed out before the pounding can begin. Though food preparation is solely women's work, the basketware implements, which often bear bold designs, are considered an art form and are made by the men.

Using a vertical loom, a young Waura woman knots cotton thread around strands of palm-leaf fibre to make a hammock, the traditional Indian bed. The hammocks are slung from poles in the communal thatch houses, the wife's under her husband's. The loom is also used to weave anklets and hipbands worn as decoration. Clothes are unknown and the Indians take pride in their nakedness. The women often emphasize it by plucking their pubic hair and sometimes their eyebrows as well.

Eyes tightly closed, a Maku baby submits to a cold shower poured by his solicitous mother from a calabash shell.

Waura Indians in the bows of dugout canoes stir the water to frighten fish into nets held by their partners in the sterns.

Fishing Without Hooks

There is such a profusion of fish in the Amazon rivers that after mandioca, the Indians eat more fish than anything else. They have no hooks, but their own fishing methods, if primitive by European standards, work surprisingly well.

In shallow backwaters where innumerable fish rest close to the bottom, the men simply stir up the river water with long poles. When fish start swimming towards the surface in fright, they are scooped up in nets or baskets of palm-leaf fibre, held sometimes by the men in canoes or perhaps by the women and children waiting on the banks.

Another method, though less often used, is even more effective. The fishermen thrash an area of enclosed water with poisonous vines until the surface is blue from the juice released by their actions. Then they wait with their nets and baskets as the trapped fish grow numb, die and float to the surface.

When the catch fails, as it often does in the rainy season, the Amazon Indians sometimes attempt to charm the fish back. They may swing carved, wooden blades on string, devices known to anthropologists as bull-roarers, because they make a noise like a bull bellowing, or they may sink a magical stone in the water, in the hope that this will summon the fish. More prosaically, the Indians supplement their otherwise monotonous food supply by gathering fruit and hunting game.

A chief of the Suya tribe, wearing a lip disc, strings fish on a vine for carrying.

An Erigbaagtsa Indian carries a palm-wood bow, bamboo arrows and a basket of palm leaves on a hunt for bush turkeys in the Upper Xingu. There, as elsewhere in the Amazon, game is scarce and he has to trick his prey, using the leaves as camouflage while he imitates the bird's call sign.

A Trumai child, also from the Upper Xingu, gazes spellbound at his catch, a large spider. His metal-tipped arrow has been provided by the Brazilian government which, since 1962, has encouraged hunting and has opened reservations for tribes, like the Trumai, that are now almost extinct.

Waura Indians wait for monkey or deer to flee a patch of flaming vegetation. Starting fires as a technique of hunting is common in the relatively dry savannah region of the Upper Xingu, but the practice is not emulated elsewhere. The tribes of the Upper Amazon, for example, rely on the blowgun, a hollowed wooden tube up to 16 feet long that is a highly effective weapon. Using arrows tipped with the vegetable poison, curare, they can kill animals as far as 120 feet away.

7/ The Threatened Land

When the rumour of man and his machines dies away, then the voice of Nature comes into its own.

KONRAD GUENTHER/A NATURALIST IN BRAZIL

During my stay in the middle Amazon. I travelled south in a light plane to the working-face of the Trans-Amazonian Highway near Humaitá on the river Madeira. The highway rakes through the red earth of the southern Amazon region as if the forest had been scratched by a giant cat. We landed on a wide part of the road. In the distance one could hear the puny roar of bulldozers, and jeeps passed back and forth to the work camp; on either side of us the forest was mangled and chewed. Roots clawed the air. The barren earth was flanked by unbroken walls of vegetation almost 150 feet high. They too would soon be flattened. Already more than 50,000 square miles of forest have been cut down and burned. At this rate of destruction the Brazilian rain forest may virtually disappear within 50 years.

The highway is the latest of many attempts—mostly failures—to tame the forest. It may open much of the jungle to lumbering, mining and cattle raising. Its first aim, however, is to promote farming. By the mid-1960s more than 50,000 colonizers had appeared along the section of Trans-Amazonian highway between Maraba and Altamire, settled in communities of about 2,000 people. These settlements are planned every 10 miles along the highway and the surrounding land is divided into 40 acre plots for agricultural development. By the end of the decade more than 400,000 pioneers will have arrived at the "new farming frontiers", mostly from the north-east of the country. Promotional literature speaks of "fertile valleys", and "a thick layer of humus accumulated during centuries", implying that this rich forest will produce equally rich crops.

This development programme seems to take for granted that food crops will grow just as easily as the luxuriant forest vegetation that they are replacing. But most of the rain forest will never be suitable for agriculture without a continuous investment in fertilizers on an economically ruinous scale. The Indians could add their pennyworth to the debate—they have been farming in the forest for thousands of years, with pitiful results. They have generally used the slash-and-burn method. A plot is chosen, trees are cut down and allowed to dry, and then burnt. The ash serves as fertilizer for a few years—usually two, or three with luck—and then the farmer moves on. This method is admirably suited to the environment, provided the farming population remains at a very low level. Areas temporarily carved out of the jungle for cultivation are insignificant in size; they are surrounded by trees that have no difficulty repopulating them when man has gone.

Something similar to the slash-and-burn method of agriculture was used in Europe ten or twelve thousand years ago, when that continent— at least in the summertime—probably bore a superficial resemblance to the Amazon region now. But there was a difference. When shifting agriculture gave way to the permanently settled kind in Europe, the land was found to be rich and steadily productive even without its forest cover. In most of the Amazon region this has not been the case.

I was able to observe the pathetic results of Indian agriculture on my visit to Cujubim Falls on the Upper Catrimani. The Indians living in one large communal *maloca* had cut out gardens from the forest, and were growing mandioca and bananas, as well as a little cotton and tobacco. They gave me a guide to lead me along the half-hour walk through the forest to tour one of their gardens.

My guide and I had no words in common; more serious was the fact that we seemed to have no attitudes in common. The young man was about 15 or 16 years old and perhaps he was uncomfortably aware of a generation gap, as well as other gaps. He had been instructed to show me his family's garden and he was doing so, with no bad grace, but with the obedient resignation of a boy doing a chore. He hardly noticed when I toppled from a log bridge and wet myself to the waist in a forest stream. It may have been inconceivable to him that any quite ancient person could accidentally slip off a tree no more than five inches in diameter. He may have thought that I had some eccentric reason for doing this

—some unfathomable whim—and that it was polite not to notice.

Walking behind my guide across the baked earth of the garden, I noticed that it was criss-crossed by a number of felled and sometimes fire-charred trees. Very little attempt had been made at weeding, and the planting was most disordered. It was extremely hot, oppressive and dismal. In striking contrast, the forest from which we had just come was cool and inviting. In short, it was just the reverse of what a person from a temperate climate would normally think of as a garden. It was a place from which one would have to *escape* for comfort.

But I knew that these agricultural methods—however slovenly they looked to me—were not irrational here. Weeding, for instance, which decreases competition from non-food plants, also lays the ground open to erosion and leaching. The ground here was eroded and leached enough as it was. The charred, decomposing tree trunks, which made it impossible to walk across the area in a straight line, nevertheless returned something to the soil; possibly they also served as decoys for pests. In any case, as the land could rarely be cultivated for more than two or three years, energy was more properly spent in preparing new plots, or in searching for other sources of food.

There was consequently not very much to see here; the garden was an absence rather than a presence. But as we walked back into the welcoming jungle I realized—I think for the first time—that what I had seen was not so much primitive as it was adaptive. Methods of agriculture, here, were as adjusted to the environment as the practice of planting in the spring in Europe, or not ploughing frozen fields.

The danger of ignoring slowly developed adaptations, of introducing methods alien to the environment, was impressed on me when I was visiting another part of the Amazon, east of Belém, where men of a European culture had decided to improve on the Indians' shifting, slash-and-burn type of agriculture and had met with something very close to disaster. Belém, the largest city in the Amazon with well over 800,000 people, lies on the river Pará, the southernmost and lesser of the Amazon's two outlets to the Atlantic. East of it, between the river Guama and the coast, is the Bragantina Zone, an area of about 12,000 square miles that was colonized towards the end of the last century by immigrants from Brazil's populous and drought-striken north-east. As one of them said when he arrived in his new home: "A place where it rains every day—this is all I ask!"

He should have asked for more. The rather haphazardly planned purpose of this colonization was to provide the growing city of Belém with foodstuffs. The Bragantina area was covered with typical *terra firme* rain forest. It was only logical, therefore, to suppose that land which produced such masses of greenery could easily supply a city with food. Tracts of high jungle were ruthlessly cut down and mandioca, corn, beans, rice and tobacco were planted. Within a few years the first cultivated lands were exhausted: but there were plenty more, and the axes bit deeper and deeper into the jungle. By 1908, a railway was built and there was a kind of agricultural boom, with tens of thousands of people rushing in to conquer the forest.

By 1950 all primary jungle was down and farmers had long since turned back on the secondary growth. Culturally, they were adapted to fixed agriculture; after the previously cultivated land had lain fallow for a few years they returned to it. The second time round, however, cutting and burning brought fertility for only one year—a third cutting was hardly worth the effort.

The people of the Bragantina Zone have not only failed to produce food for Belém: they can hardly support themselves and now import much of their basic diet. Economically speaking, at least, the area is practically sterile; and the railway has stopped running. Population density is still over 12 persons per square mile (as against under one per square mile in the rest of the Amazon) and the government is now trying to move people out, not in. Many are also moving out of their own accord: in two decades the population of Belém almost tripled, a good part of the increase coming from an influx of refugees from a forest that has become, for all practical purposes, a desert.

The odd thing is that the Bragantina Zone still *looks* gloriously fertile. As we drove out on a well-kept but rather deserted highway the fields and scrub on all sides were bright green. At one point we came to a Japanese pepper plantation, which seemed to be thriving; but, as we learned, each of the plants was set in what amounted to a little pot of relatively good earth, which had been trucked in. Furthermore, the pepper plants were beginning to be attacked by disease.

It is now known that the Amazon forest's fertility is a response to climate and not to the richness of the soil. The substances necessary for plant life circulate through plants themselves, not through the soil. So when the forest is cut down and burned, these vital substances are also destroyed. Almost all of the nitrogen and sulphur go up in smoke. Most of the carbon goes the same way. What remains as wood

A burned section of forest makes space for agriculture. Ash acts as fertilizer, but the land stays productive for only two or three years.

ash is soon washed away by the rain. Any fertility left disappears with the first crop that is harvested. There may be no second crop.

The human price paid by those who ignore these facts of forest ecology was brought home to me by what I saw during my tour of the Bragantina Zone. We came on a deserted plantation house, standing like a baroque ghost just off the highway. It had been an impressive villa about 50 years ago; but now massive lianas had thrust through the stained-glass windows, the floors had dropped out around rotting, moss-hung beams. New trees had sprung up in the debris on the cracked foundation, and were poking through the tattered roof. The jungle was coming back, much more vigorously here in the old living-quarters than in the abandoned outlying fields, which supported only green scrub. Nowhere else in the Amazon did I feel the massive, maternal strength of the forest as strongly as here.

There is one area on the southern edge of the Amazon rain forest, the Mato Grosso, where the vegetation has been cleared and where a different kind of food appears to grow in abundance: beef. Cattle ranches have been set up rapidly, and by the 1970s more than 10 million cattle were in residence.

This rapid expansion of the beef industry is almost entirely the result of private enterprise, and not careful government planning. In the late fifties and early sixties, the government sold empty squares on the map of Mato Grosso for a nominal fee to speculators. The forest was cut down and burned. Buildings were erected. Special grass was sown that suppressed other vegetation and provided food for the cattle. The ranch owners will make money whether they sell their beef or not— their profit comes from tax relief and capital gains—but the forgotten land under the feet of 10 million cattle may be of little value to anyone in the future. Fertility is being reduced and erosion has begun. The true environmental cost of such exploitation has yet to be calculated.

The present destruction of the rain forest seems to be benefiting very few people so far. But the new road network is providing access to areas of forest that have until recently concealed undisputed riches— gold, diamonds and numerous minerals such as manganese, bauxite, iron, tin, copper and lead, and other metals. There is every prospect that mining companies in Brazil will be in full operation in the rock shield areas on either side of the river Amazon by the 1980s. Enormous deposits of industrial metals have been found here. There is no point in attempting to list them all because it is very possible that many of the most important deposits are being kept secret. As an indication of the magnitude of these finds, however, in the Serra dos Carajas, between the Xingu and the Tocantins rivers, geologists working for U.S. Steel have located what may be one of the largest reserves of iron ore in the world: a possible 30,000 million tons.

Of all projects designed to exploit the Amazon probably those involving mining have the greatest financial justification. And from a purely environmental point of view, mining may well be the least disruptive of man's present efforts to develop the Amazon. Although the mineral deposits in the region are enormous, they occupy relatively small areas. The iron ore in the Serra dos Carajas, for instance, is found in an area of approximately 1,000 square miles (many cattle ranches in the Mato Grosso are much bigger). When the mining comes to an end, the forest's wounds will heal over. Although mining is not a permanent solution—these resources eventually become exhausted also—it may be the best way of accommodating, feeding and providing jobs for the three million annual additions to Brazil's population.

There are those who disagree, of course: some scientists feel that there are strong arguments for preserving the forest and exploiting its timber rather than the land or minerals beneath. But Amazonian timber is tricky to exploit. In a heterogeneous forest with literally thousands of species of trees, only a fraction of the species are commercially useful—one estimate runs as low as five per cent. Of these there may also be only one or two individuals of any useful size per square mile. Furthermore, the world timber markets are almost exclusively geared to soft woods, and the incidence of all soft wood trees in the *terra firme* primary forest is seldom even ten per cent.

However, there is just a possibility—by no means a certainty—that modern man can edge his way in here and, by doing so, paradoxically relax his relentless pressure on the jungle. This possibility depends on the fact that primary and secondary growths in the forest are not antithetical but complementary, and that light-loving secondary growths are generally trees of soft wood which grow quickly in forest clearings. If it were therefore possible to arrest parts of the jungle at a secondary level, planting commercially useful trees, there would be plenty of room for primary growth as well.

I visited a vast experimental tree farm at Monte Dourado on the river Jari for several days. It was run by an unmistakably North American firm—iced water on the dining room tables, lavishly abundant and some-what over-cooked food, rrrrasped Inglish, and a scientific approach to

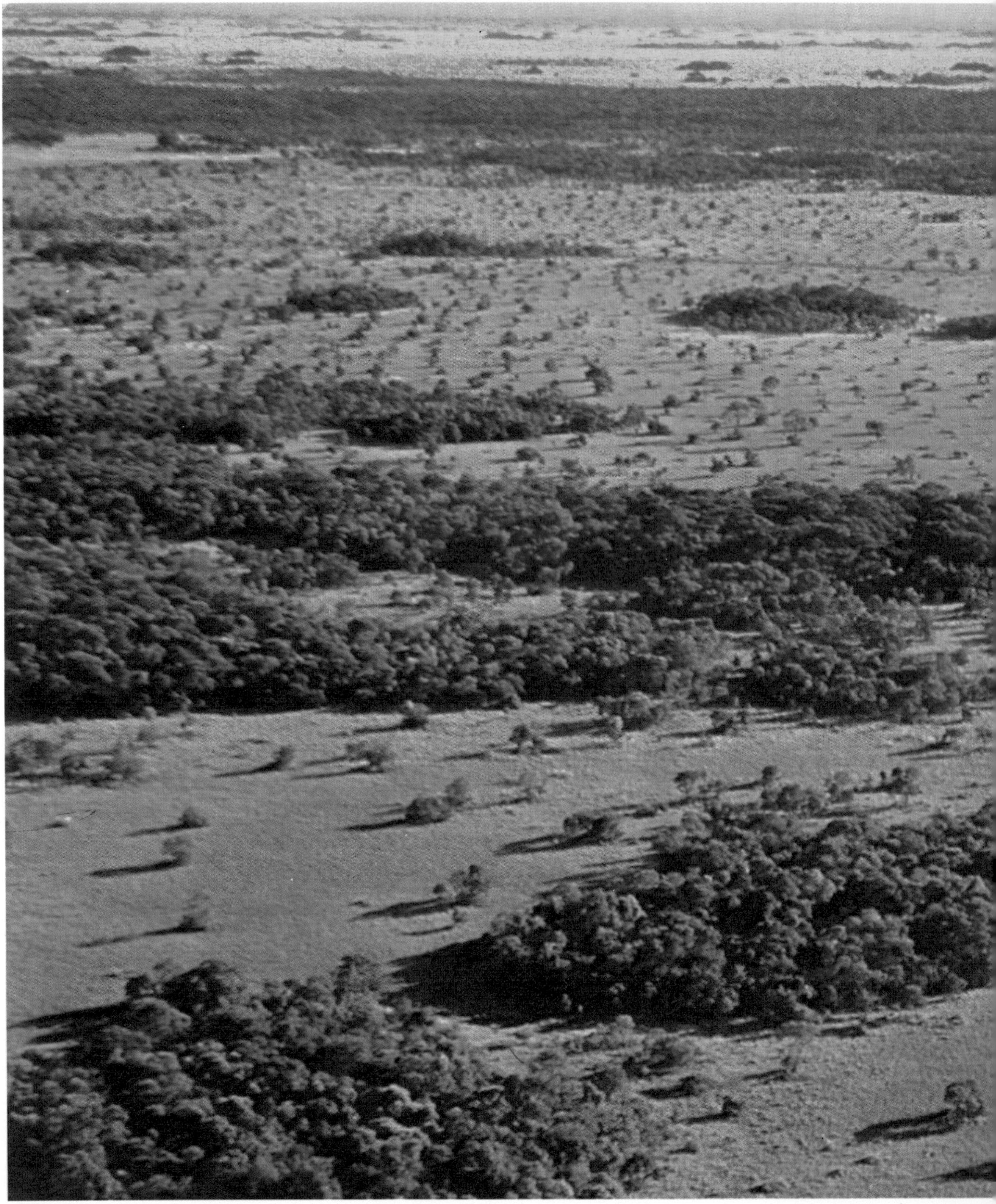

Islands of trees dot the savannah at the forest's edge. The surprising sharpness of the border is created by animal grazing or fires.

a tricky problem worthy of a moon-shot. It was clear that if anyone would succeed in taming at least a part of the rain forest without destroying it, these people would.

Essentially, the project was to lay down stands of exotic soft wood trees suitable for making paper amid brakes of virgin forest. The trees, raised from seed, were exotic because they were less likely to be attacked by local diseases and parasites. Aside from the fact that the operation was run with obvious efficiency, and with every mechanical and scientific tool known to man, I am in no position to say whether it was, or will be, a success or failure. But the very armaments that had been brought up to face the hostile forest were an indication of the magnitude of the problem. It is not possible to escape a certain feeling of tension, here, as though the researchers were in a forward command post, with armies of diseases and parasites lurking beyond the peri-meter in the dark jungle. Once again I felt the jealous power of this giant, intertwining mass of vegetation. Very soon, it will be seen whether the 20th Century's methods of exploiting the forest are more effective than those of the Indians, whether modern man can tame the wilderness or must accept it and learn to live with it.

One day, on the Upper Cujeiras, I saw a remarkable example of a man totally and successfully adapted to a forest existence. I came on the river-side shack of an old hunter. There are a number of these men living alone in the back tributaries. Usually, they are almost pure Indian, although they are completely detribalized. The few that I saw seemed to have dropped out of the human race altogether, and they were not very unhappy about their choice. They all had dogs, and this one had two. Both these animals had adapted so well to the life of their master that they looked like him: they were lean and hard, and there was something intensely placid about them. They obeyed the hunter's every word, as more domesticated dogs never learn to do, but they never cringed or whined. Like their master, also, they were somehow neat and orderly, without seeming to be so. They had appointed places to sleep in the sun (or shade, depending on the time of day) and places to stand on the river bank looking noble, and precise positions to take in the hunter's dugout canoe in order to balance it properly. I have never seen more contented dogs, though they were also highly keyed and immensely eager to hunt.

The man must have been in his middle fifties. He had the brown, wrinkled knees and elbows of the aged, but he was as tough as mahogany and could obviously have walked the legs off most men half his age. The muscles of his arms and thighs and belly were flat and unobtrusive, shaped for endurance. Quite obviously, his diet was protein, and he drove himself as hard as his prey to get it. We talked for a while; he was full of apologies because he had no coffee, an almost unforgivable sin for a Brazilian host. Aside from coffee, however, he appeared to want nothing. His little house was almost old-maidishly trim; a better word, perhaps, would be ship-shape—sailors can be old-maidish too.

Every few days this happy man would go into the jungle with his dogs to hunt. There, he found sufficient food for himself, and for them, and once in a while he took a pelt which he sold (illegally) down river. It was enough. Indeed, as I could see with a certain envy, it was more than enough; he was a very rich man with his neat house and his neat dogs and all the time in the world—which, I saw with another twinge of envy, did not weigh on his hands at all. Like the dogs, he was thoroughly enjoying himself, though he could have used some coffee.

I asked the hunter, then, if he had ever been married—clearly he lived alone here now. It seemed another thing that he might be missing, even more than coffee, perhaps. No, he said, he had never lived with a woman and did not intend to. Women, he said, were too messy, and made too much noise. Anyway, he added, "I am married to her." With this, he pointed to the great forest behind him. On the surface, it was an ordinary remark, much as a man might say that he was married to his work. But I could see that he took the statement very seriously. That is to say, he took the *gender* of the forest seriously. For him, it was a woman, and not a virginal woman either. She was the guardian of the creatures he hunted. Indeed, when he spoke of hunting, he had the settled look of a happily married man. His wife was clean, efficient and reliable if treated with proper respect.

As we shoved off in our boat, the hunter stood on a spit of sand with his two proud dogs and waved goodbye. Then with apparent relief, he walked back into what he surely believed was the eternal forest.

Patterns of the Amazon

Despite its monotonous green, the Amazon has an astonishing ability to stimulate the imaginations of those who explore it. It is fortunate that among the great scientist-explorers were men with fertile minds who were capable of describing what they saw with extraordinary vividness. The Victorian botanist, Richard Spruce, for example, wrote of the giant Victoria Amazonica water lily: "The impression the plant gave me, when viewed from the bank above, was that of a number of green teatrays floating, with here and there a bouquet protruding between them; but when more closely surveyed the leaves excited the utmost admiration, from their immensity and perfect symmetry. A leaf turned up," continued Spruce, "suggests some strange fabric of cast iron, just taken from the furnace, its ruddy colour and the enormous ribs with which it is strengthened, increasing the symmetry."

Nowadays many of these almost theatrical effects can be captured by the camera, as the photographs on these pages demonstrate. What seems to be a hairy carpet is in fact a mass of crawling caterpillars. A weird sculpture looking like a skyscraper with musical notes for windows is only a palm leaf chewed by hungry insects and lit by the sun. Ribbed sandbanks look like abstract art. The magnified veins of a palm leaf are transformed into converging railway tracks and raindrops become crystals upon a leafy background. Gleaming undulations are, in fact, the river Negro's surface.

Similes and metaphors of this sort have proved themselves to be a much favoured way of describing the aesthetic qualities of the Amazon. Henry Walter Bates, the better known contemporary of Spruce, used them generously. The lianas in the forest, he noticed, "were twisted in strands like cables; others had thick stems contorted in every variety and shape, entwining snake-like round the tree trunks; others again were of zig-zag shape, or indented like the steps of a staircase sweeping from the ground to a giddy height."

No doubt the very fact that the mysteries are hidden is what sets the imagination free. In the end, explorers begin to see the wilderness as a live creature whose inner life is suppressed by the mantle of green but shines through even the palest flower and pours itself out into the powerful currents of the rivers flooding down to the sea.

RIVER BED SANDBANKS IN THE DRY SEASON

RAINDROPS ON A LOTUS LEAF

LEAVES OF THE VICTORIA AMAZONICA LILY

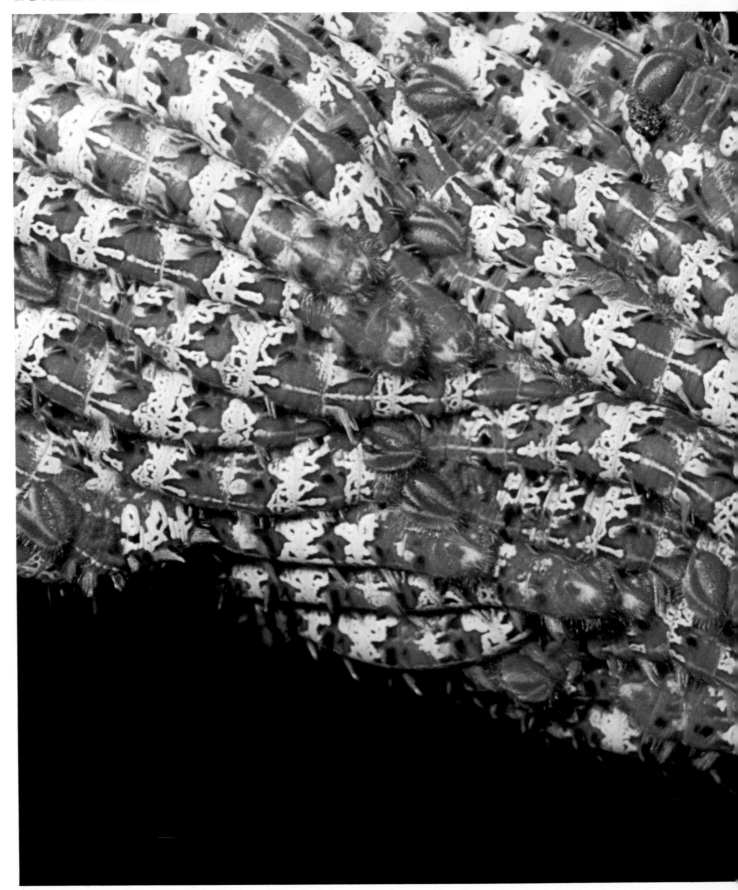

CATERPILLARS CRAWLING ALONG A TREE TRUNK

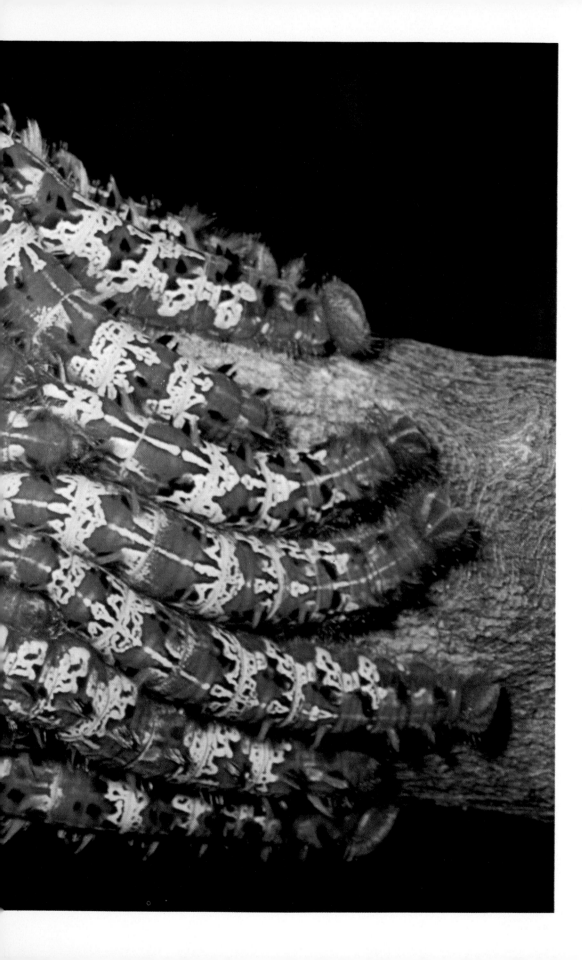

MAGNIFIED VEINS OF A PALM LEAF

A PALM LEAF EATEN BY INSECTS

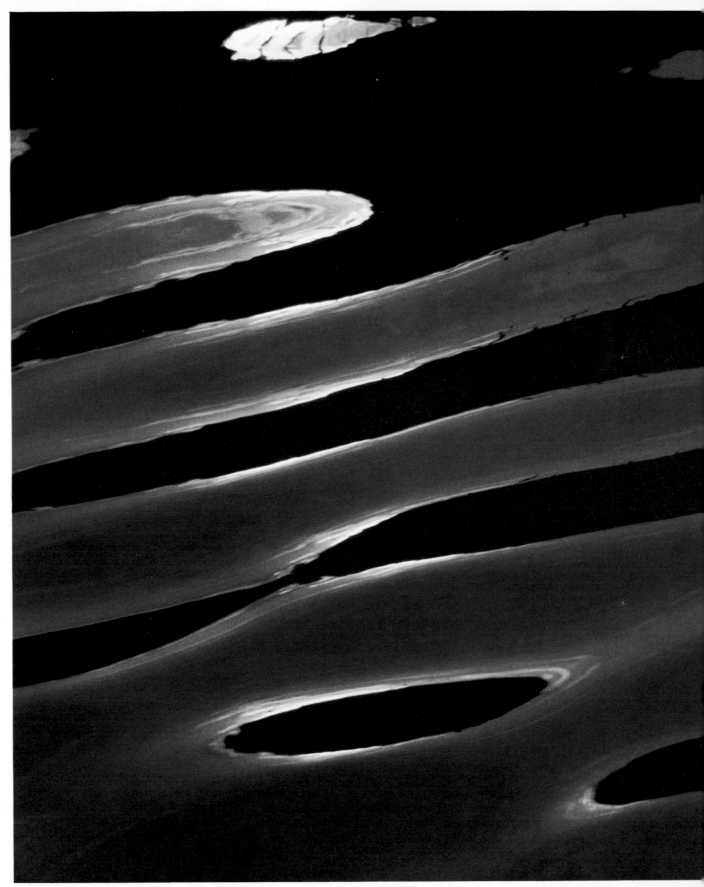

THE DARK WATERS OF THE RIVER NEGRO AT SUNSET

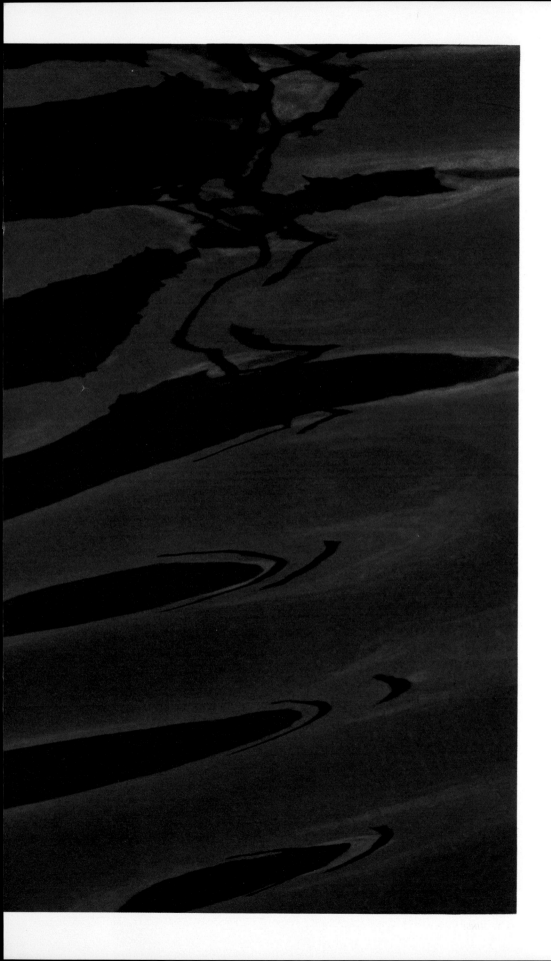

Bibliography

Adams, Alexander B., *The Eternal Quest.* Constable, 1970.

Barcant, Malcolm, *Field Guide to Butterflies of Trinidad and Tobago.* Collins, 1970.

Bates, Henry Walter, *The Naturalist on The River Amazons.* University of California Press, 1962; Dent, 1969.

Bates, Marston, *The Land and Wildlife of South America.* Time-Life International (Nederland) NV, 1969.

Beddall, Barbara G., (Ed.), *Wallace and Bates in the Tropics.* Collier-Macmillan, 1970.

Bodard, Lucien, *Massacre on the Amazon.* Tom Stacey, 1971.

Burns, E. Bradford, *A Documentary History of Brazil.* Alfred A. Knopf, 1970.

Dorst, Jean, *South America, A Natural History.* Hamish Hamilton, 1967.

Fleming, Peter, *Brazilian Adventure.* Jonathan Cape, 1968.

Furneaux, Robin, *The Amazon.* Hamish Hamilton, 1969.

Garner, H. F., *Tropical Weathering and Relief,* Vol. III *The Encyclopaedia of Geomorphology.* Ed. Rhodes W. Fairbridge, Van Noost Reinhold, 1969.

Gibbs, Ronald J., *The Geochemistry of the Amazon River System.* Geological Society of America, Bulletin 1967.

Gibbs, Ronald J., *Circulation in the Amazon River Estuary and Adjacent Atlantic Ocean.* Journal of Marine Research, Vol. 28, 2, 1970.

Guenther, Konrad, *A Naturalist in Brazil.* George, Allen and Unwin, 1931.

Guppy, Nicholas, *Wai-Wai.* John Murray, 1958.

Von Hagen, Victor Wolfgang, *South America Called Them.* Alfred A. Knopf, 1945.

Von Hagen, Victor Wolfgang, *South America, The Green World of the Naturalists.* Eyre and Spottiswoode, 1951.

Hanbury-Tenison, Robin, *A Question of Survival.* Angus and Robertson, 1973.

Karsten, Raphael, *The Civilization of the South American Indians.* Dawsons Pall Mall, 1968.

Klinge, H., *Podzol Soils in the Amazon Basin.* Journal of Sciences, 16: pp. 95-103, 1965.

Lathrap, Donald W., *The Upper Amazon.* Thames and Hudson, 1970.

Maybury-Lewis, David, *The Savage and the Innocent.* Evans Bros. Ltd., 1965.

Meggers, Betty J., *Amazonia.* Aldine-Atherton, Inc., 1971.

Myers, G. S., *The Amazon and its Fishes.* Parts 1-4 Aquarium Journal 18:(3):4-9; (4):13-20; (5):6-13; 32; (7):8-19, 34.

Richards, P. W., *The Tropical Rain Forest: an Ecological Study.* Cambridge University Press, 1952.

Schreider, Helen and Frank, *Exploring the Amazon.* National Geographic Society, 1970.

Schulthess, Emil, *The Amazon.* Simon and Schuster, 1962.

De Shauensee, Rodolphe Meyer, *A Guide to the Birds of South America.* Oliver and Boyd, 1970.

Sioli, H. *General Features of the Delta of the Amazon.* Proceedings of the Dacca Symposium UNESCO 1966:381-390.

Sioli, H. *Hydrochemistry and Geology in the Brazilian Amazon Region.* Amazoniana, Vol. 1, (3). Kommissions-Verlag Walter G. Muhlau Kiel, 1968.

Smith, Anthony, *Matto Grosso, Last Virgin Land.* Michael Joseph, 1971.

Spruce, Richard, *Amazon and Andes.* Macmillan, 1908.

Spruce, Richard, *Notes of a Botanist on the Amazon and Andes.* Macmillan, 1908.

Steward, Julian H., *Handbook of South American Indians.* U.S. Government Printing Office, 1948.

Wagley, Charles, *An Introduction to Brazil.* Columbia University Press, 1971.

Wallace, Alfred Russel, *Narrative of Travels on the Amazon and the Rio Negro.* Reeve and Co., 1905.

Woodcock, George, *Henry Walter Bates: Naturalist of the Amazons.* Faber and Faber, 1969.

Acknowledgements

The author and editors of this book wish to thank the following: Mrs. Claudia Andujar; Dr. Miguel Alves de Lima, Instituto Brasiliero de Geografia, Rio de Janeiro; Dr. Jorge Ronaldo Barbosa, Itamarati, Brasilia; Dr. Lucio de Castro Soares, Instituto Brasiliero de Geografia, Rio de Janeiro; Dr. Carlos Chagas, Rio de Janeiro; Donna Clara, Librarian at the Museu Paraense Emilio Goeldi, Belém; Steven Corry, Survival International; Nicole Duplaix-Hall, The Zoological Society of London; Dr. Luiz Fernando Costa Bomfim, Bôa Vista; Vice-Admiral Francisco Ferreira Netto, Rio de Janeiro; Professor Manuel Frota Moreira, Director General, Departamento Técnico Científico do Conselho Nacional de Pesquisas, Rio de Janeiro; Brian Gould, Abril Press, São Paulo; Dr. Ney Oscar de Lima Rayol, Brasilia; Officials of The Daniel Ludwig Bulk Carriers Experimental Tree Farm at Monte Dourado, Jari River; Professor Paulo Machado, National Council of Amazonian Researches, Manáus; Dr. Giuseppe Mezzasalma, Tratores Fiat do Brasil, Rio de Janeiro; Missionaries at the Salesian Mission, Manáus; Officials of the National Department of Highways in Rio de Janeiro and in Manáus; Dr. Jovinho de Oliveira, Rio de Janeiro; Dr. Elio Peccei, Director-President, Tratores Fiat do Brasil, Rio de Janeiro; W. A. Pereira, Director-President, Centrales Eléctricas do Amazonas S.A., Manáus; Professor Marilio Pires Domingues, Assessoria Especial de Relações Públicas da Presidência da República, Rio de Janeiro; The Bishop of Roraima, Prelazia, Bôa Vista; Dr. Gilberta Ben Sabath, Instituto Evandro Chagas, Belém; Father Giovanni Saffirio, Missionary on the Upper Catrimani in the Roraima Territory; Peter Searle, London; Dr. Jeffrey J. Shaw, Instituto Evandro Chagas, Belém; Anthony Smith, Fellow of the Zoological Society, London; John B. Thornes, London.

Index

Numerals in italics indicate a photograph or drawing of the subject mentioned.

XXX

Colour reproduction by
Printing Developments International Ltd.,
Leeds, England—a Time Inc. subsidiary
Filmsetting by C. E. Dawkins (Typesetters) Ltd., London.
Printed by Smeets Lithographers, Weert.
Bound by Proost en Brandt N.V., Amsterdam
Printed in Holland